GHOSTS
OF THE
BIG SUR COAST

GHOSTS
OF THE
BIG SUR COAST

Randall A. Reinstedt

Ghost Town Publications
Carmel, California

For other books by Randall A. Reinstedt, see page 85. If book-stores in your area do not carry these titles, copies may be obtained by writing to . . .

Ghost Town Publications
P.O. Drawer 5998 ◆ Carmel, CA 93921
www.ghosttownpub.com

For photo credits see pages 83–84

10 9 8 7 6 5

This work is an expanded version of the book *Incredible Ghosts of the Big Sur Coast*, published in 1981.

Manufactured in the United States of America

ISBN 0-933818-11-4
Library of Congress Control Number: 2002092065

Edited by John Bergez
Cover and maps by Ed Greco
Typesetting by Erick and Mary Ann Reinstedt

Cover: For the story of the antique aircraft that has been seen, and heard, flying under Bixby Bridge on Coast Highway One, see "A ghostly airplane of World War I vintage . . . ," page 34.

Oval illustration, pages ix, 1, 5, 79, 81, 83: This photograph shows a portion of the once thriving coastal community of Not-ley's Landing—truly a ghost of the past. For additional pictures see page 36. For Notley's Landing information, see pages 25–26.

To Reiny and his friends,
who knew the coast better than most

GHOSTS
OF THE BIG SUR COAST

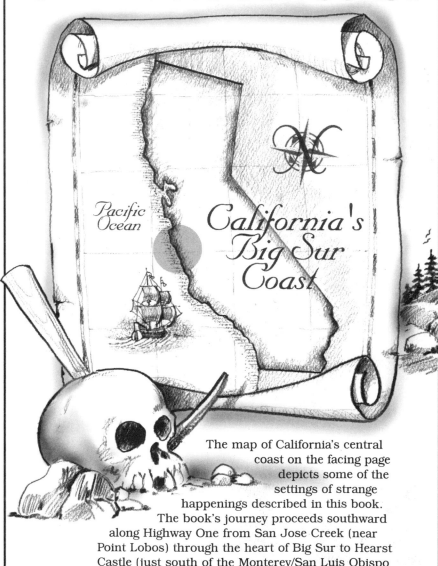

Pacific
Ocean

California's
Big Sur
Coast

The map of California's central
coast on the facing page
depicts some of the
settings of strange
happenings described in this book.
The book's journey proceeds southward
along Highway One from San Jose Creek (near
Point Lobos) through the heart of Big Sur to Hearst
Castle (just south of the Monterey/San Luis Obispo
County line).

Monterey Bay

Monterey Peninsula

Carmel Bay

CARMELITE MONASTERY

POINT LOBOS

SAN JOSE CREEK

CARMEL HIGHLANDS

PALO COLORADO CANYON

BIXBY BRIDGE

LITTLE SUR RIVER

PICO BLANCO

PFEIFFER BIG SUR STATE PARK

POINT SUR

POST HOUSE

MACON

MISSION SAN ANTONIO

CAPE SAN MARTIN

WILLOW CREEK

MASSACRE CAVE

LOS BURROS MINING DISTRICT

HEARST CASTLE

Pacific Ocean

MONTEREY COUNTY
SAN LUIS OBISPO COUNTY

Contents

Introduction

The Big Sur coast is one of the world's most beautiful areas. Among its attractions are its magnificent mountains, unsurpassed vistas, picturesque valleys, treacherous canyons, ageless redwoods, and, perhaps most breathtaking of all, its rugged shoreline. Add to this such tantalizing things as hidden beaches, secluded surfing sites, remote hiking trails, lost treasures, neglected gold mines, historic shipwrecks, cliff-clinging roads, and world-class restaurants and accommodations, and it is little wonder this Pacific paradise is one of California's most popular vacation destinations.

For most visitors, Big Sur is inextricably linked with Highway One, the spectacular, winding road that hugs the central coast, turning inland to pass through Big Sur Valley and its tiny village. This stretch of California's coastal highway has been described by travelers from around the globe as one of the world's most awe-inspiring roads. Having "starred" in numerous films and television productions (including many commercials), the central coast road has also been celebrated in various publications as "the most beautiful drive in the nation," "the best of the best" (when judged against the country's most scenic roads), "the American Amalfi" and, according to the federal Department of Transportation, one of only six "All American Roads."

Yet few who wend their way along Highway One to admire the natural wonders of Big Sur are aware of the area's *unnatural* heritage as the home to scores of strange tales of ghosts and other out-of-the-ordinary happenings. Together with many events of more traditional historic importance, such accounts are part of the legacy of Big Sur, and they only add to our appreciation of this land of wild beauty and dark secrets.

To appreciate the Big Sur of today, we must look at yesterday, and a time when only Native Americans occupied the land. Intimately intertwined with the lore of this wilderness region are the tales told by these first settlers. Among their accounts are stories of such things as a sacred mountain, mysterious gathering places, healing hot springs, and chambers of gold. While I find all of these fascinating, my favorite tale dating back to these times tells of a huge natural cavern adorned with pictures of beasts that roamed the land long before humans are supposed to have arrived in these parts. (A detailed account of this "underground world" is in the text.)

In time, Spanish explorers and men of God found their way to this Pacific paradise. With them came change. Sadly, other than the cross, and what they believed was a more civilized way of life, the newcomers also brought disease. For the native people of California, this invasion from faraway lands signaled the end of the culture and way of life they loved.

The changes brought by the Spanish also included names. Among them was El Pais Grande del Sur, meaning "The Big Country to the South" (south of Alta California's capital city of Monterey and its nearby mission). This name, most agree, was eventually shortened to the more familiar Big Sur (Big South) that we know today.

As to where the "Big South" begins and ends, one can only shake his head and say, "¿Quién sabe?" (Who knows?). For some, especially casual visitors to the area, Big Sur means only the Pfeiffer Big Sur State Park, which is mostly nestled in the Big Sur Valley. For those at the other end of the spectrum, and who are also unfamiliar with the region, Big Sur includes all the land between the coastal community of Carmel and the town of Cambria, approximately 100 twisting highway miles to the south. Somewhere in between is the real Big Sur.

For the purposes of this publication I have chosen my own Big Sur boundaries. When I refer to the Big Sur coast, I am thinking of the land between San Jose Creek (to the north, near beautiful Point Lobos State Reserve) and Salmon Creek (to the south, near the Monterey/San Luis Obispo County line and the southern extremities of the Los Burros Mining District).

This stretch of land is said to rival any shoreline in the world for breathtaking vistas. But there is more to Big Sur than its scenic wonders. This seventy-plus mile stretch along central California's cliff-clinging coastal highway also boasts a multitude of colorful characters and intriguing tales. Included in this plethora of local lore are scores of stories of ghosts, peculiar happenings, and haunting mysteries.

It is these tales of the strange and unexplained—mixed with a smattering of local history—that this book is about.

I originally published a version of this book in 1981. Since then a number of new stories have come my way, making it more than worthwhile to expand and update the book. For the sake of completeness, I have also included versions of some accounts related to the Big Sur area that have appeared in my other works. My hope is that bringing all these stories together in one publication, including many that have never before been published, will lead both residents and visitors alike to appreciate Big Sur, its people, and its colorful heritage all the more.

In closing, I would like to welcome everyone to Big Sur. Whether you are reading this work from afar, or are using it as a guide as you travel central California's scenic shoreline, I hope your journey is a pleasant one and that you will return again and again to this magical land of beautiful vistas and intriguing tales.

Randall A. Reinstedt

Ghosts of the Big Sur Coast

The journey begins . . .

As discussed in the Introduction, for the purposes of this publication the Big Sur coast's northern boundary begins at picturesque San Jose Creek. For those unfamiliar with California's Monterey County coast, San Jose Creek is near the beautiful Point Lobos State Reserve and is slightly south of the famed Monterey Peninsula (see map, page vii). Those who plan to journey south from the Monterey-Carmel area—whether it be a vicarious trip within the confines of this book, or a winding drive along the coast's spectacular Highway One—are in for a treat.

With San Jose Creek as a starting point, one of the West's most scenic and interesting areas begins to unfold. As the text of this book works its way southward from San Jose Creek down the rugged coastline, a variety of ghostly occurrences, unexplained happenings, and interesting glimpses into the area's history will be explored.

San Jose Creek winds its way to its outlet in Carmel Bay at a spot known as Monastery Beach. Also known as San Jose Creek Beach, this location is part of a coastal stretch that is officially referred to as Carmel River State Beach. It is at Monastery Beach—some say at the mouth of San Jose Creek—that a very steep, and quite deep, submarine canyon has its beginning. Because of this canyon and the wave action it creates, as well as the spectacular underwater views it affords, the beach has become a popular—and deadly—dive location. So many divers have perished in the area that Monastery Beach has earned the ghoulish nickname of Mortuary Beach.

The Carmel Bay canyon leads to the larger and better known Monterey Submarine Canyon of Monterey Bay fame. Other than divers, the "Carmel Trench," as it is also sometimes called, attracts marine biologists and others who are interested in strange creatures of the deep. It has even been suggested that the canyon has been visited by a variety of odd and unidentifiable sea beasts that venture in and out of Carmel Bay.

Perhaps it was some as yet-unidentified beast that was responsible for the mysterious events that left scientists from far and near scratching their heads in wonder in 1994. It all began on August 24, when divers heard eerie sounds in the area of Whaler's Cove about 90 feet below the surface. (Whaler's Cove, an inlet of Carmel Bay, is part of the beautiful Point Lobos State Reserve.) The noise consisted of thump, thump, thump sounds that appeared to come at regular intervals, creating a "very low-frequency vibration" that was enough to vibrate the divers' lungs underwater.

As the noises continued to be heard, experts of various kinds, including those who study underwater acoustics, were among the droves of people who flocked to the scene. Also present were television crews from the likes of CNN and NBC's *Hard Copy.* Soon, the hubbub they created caused the activities around Point Lobos to be described as a "media circus."

Theories about the origins and nature of the sounds were nearly as plentiful as visitors to the area, with some people opting for some kind of mechanical source (such as a distant ship) and others (including at least one scientist) favoring a biological origin. But to this day, no one has conclusively explained the "massive, heartbeat-like thumping sounds" that disturbed the divers.

What is certain is that Carmel Bay's submarine canyon has been visited in the past by sizable and, in some cases, unidentified beasts of the deep. So, if you visit Monastery Beach, keep an eye out for strange creatures while you admire the view!*

Those who follow Highway One south from the Monterey Peninsula will have little trouble finding Monastery Beach. Located in a pastoral setting on the inland side of the road—and almost impossible for daytime travelers to miss—is the imposing Carmelite Monastery. It is this striking, Mediterranean-style structure, with its roof of red tiles, that gives the beach its name. A home for Carmelite nuns, the monastery is situated along the banks of San Jose Creek and overlooks Carmel Bay. Having first opened its doors in 1931—before Highway One was completed—this monument to God has graced the landscape for longer than most people can remember, and today it is considered a landmark of the Big Sur coast.

Across the creek and on a neighboring hill is a second site of importance—one that takes us considerably farther back into history than either the construction of Highway One or the opening of the Carmelite Monastery. Discovered in 1968 by a Monterey Peninsula archaeologist, the site is that of an ancient Indian village. The village is officially known as Ichxenta-ruc, but because of its close proximity to San Jose Creek, and the fact that its exact site was unknown for so many years, it is more common-

*For those who would like to learn more about the many marine oriented oddities that have become part of the legends and lore of the Monterey County coast, my book *Mysterious Sea Monsters of California's Central Coast* may be of interest. See page 85 for further information.

7

ly referred to as "The Lost Village of San Jose." Charcoal remains taken from a pit measuring more than 20 feet in depth have indicated—through carbon dating—that California Indians lit campfires there more than 2,400 years ago! As a result of long hours of excavation and research, considerably more than Indian artifacts and charcoal remains have been found at, or near, the site. Among the surprises that surfaced were the remains of an aged whaling cantina that is thought to date back to the mid 1800s. Of interest here is information stating that from 1861 to 1884 a lively, and quite profitable, whaling station was located at nearby Whaler's Cove.

While the preceding information gives some hint of the historic significance of the San Jose Creek area, this locale also enjoys another distinction, one that is more in keeping with the "spirit" of this book. For it is in this vicinity that numerous travelers have reported sighting a ghostly figure on the coast road. It is with the tale of this long-ago lady that our journey begins . . .

The mysterious matron of Monastery Beach . . .

Described in a variety of ways by both angry, and quite shaken, Highway One motorists, the "mysterious matron of Monastery Beach" has often been observed crossing the road or even walking down the middle of it. Regardless of where she happens to be, she always appears oblivious to the cars screeching to a stop around her or swerving to avoid hitting her. Lost in her own thoughts and continuing on her way, the ghostly figure is soon lost to sight. As she vanishes from view she takes with her the secret of where she came from, where she is going, who she may be, and what never-ending mission she is so intent on carrying out.

8

Interestingly, after this book was first published in 1981, I learned of two additional sightings. The first of these tales helps us to form a mental picture of the mysterious matron, while the second adds another dimension to reports of her appearances.

The first account was shared with me by the woman who experienced the sighting. Even though it took place in the late 1940s, the memory of it was still very vivid in her mind decades later. As her story begins, early one morning she was traveling south on Highway One with an elderly Carmel man. When they neared the Carmelite Monastery, they crested a hill and suddenly saw the ghostly figure of a woman walking down the middle of the road! As the driver swerved to avoid hitting her, the lady nonchalantly continued on her way as if nothing had happened. By then they were past her, and my friend stared out of the rear window as the figure slowly faded from view.

Surprised by how composed her companion was as they continued down the highway, she turned to him and asked, "How can you be so calm after almost hitting that lady?" He replied matter-of-factly, "It probably wouldn't have mattered if I *had* hit her, since she's only a ghost!"

With that he went on to say that numerous people had seen the mystery woman over the years, and he had even seen her several times himself. As to who she was, no one seemed to know. But because there was a small cemetery nearby, some suspected that she may have come from there.

In summing up her account, my friend said that the woman was dressed in "tattered" clothing and had a shawl, or scarf, partially wrapped around her head and shoulders. Her hair and clothes were "disheveled" (as perhaps one would expect from the ocean breezes), and she looked very much like a ghost (whatever that may mean).

The second tale came to my attention in 1985. Even though the story leaves much to the imagination, I can't

9

help but wonder if there might be a connection. My source for this story, a highly respected individual, had reason to be familiar with the dwelling where the tale takes place. Located between Monastery Beach and the entrance to Point Lobos State Reserve, the house is one of the oldest in the area and a Highway One landmark in its own right. It is what happens—or maybe I should say, *what is hidden*—in the house that this account is about.

Supposedly, several ghostly happenings are associated with the dwelling, most notably doors that open and close when no one is near them. But the real mystery is, what strange "thing" is kept locked in one of the basement rooms? The room is off-limits to all but the family, and its contents are never discussed with outsiders. My source left me with the distinct impression that he believed it was not something, but *someone,* who was locked away in the basement room. The mystery only deepens as the years go by, and I, for one, can't help but wonder if the mysterious matron of Monastery Beach might be able to shed some light on this Point Lobos puzzle . . .

Lost souls from a lost race . . .

Certainly puzzles abound at Point Lobos. Described as "The Greatest Meeting of Land and Water in the World," the Punta de los Lobos Marinos (Point of the Sea Wolves) is only a short walk from Monastery Beach, and harbors one of the Big Sur coast's most colorful histories.

Aside from having been won in a game of chance, the background of this beautiful place includes such things as shipwrecks, pirates, gold mines, smuggling, treasures, rum-running, abalone canning, and a profitable whaling industry. Also a part of its history are a number of strange and unexplained happenings.

Perhaps the strangest of the many tales associated with this land of myth and lore is an account about a prehistoric "race" that once dwelled on the promontory. This belief was shared by those of the occult, and the account was recorded in an aged publication about the Carmel area. As the story goes, in the dim and distant past Point Lobos was "a veritable garden of Eden." At this time it was inhabited by people of high intelligence who enjoyed lives of simplicity, security, and tranquility.

All went well for these forgotten folk until a serpent came to their Eden, bringing with it a black poison of selfishness and greed. It was this poison that brought ruin to the race. The sad tale concludes with the remarkable information that the twisted and gnarled trees that are so much a part of the picturesqueness of the scene are the reincarnation of souls of this lost race who are "doomed to haunt the shadowy places" until a race of godlike men return to the land.

Biologists would no doubt suggest a more earthly solution to the puzzle of the origin of the area's warped and wind-sculptured cypress trees, which are found nowhere in the world except on the Monterey coast. Still, anyone who has seen these famed trees clinging so tenaciously to the rocks and headlands of Point Lobos will find it easy to believe that they are indeed lost souls from a lost race, entrapped with earthbound roots and waiting for a time that may never come.

A mysterious light appeared . . .

The picturesque trees of Point Lobos also play a part in the ghostly tale of a lost shipwreck treasure. As the story goes, long ago, when Monterey was the capital of Alta (Upper) California, a Spanish vessel fell victim to a fierce Pacific storm and was dashed upon the Point Lobos rocks. Three crew members managed to escape the wreck and reach the safety of shore, each burdened with a portion of the ship's wealth.

11

Not knowing where they had landed, the newly rich threesome decided to bury their booty before setting out together to explore their surroundings. Finding themselves in a miniature forest of warped and wind-blown cypress trees, they sighted through a crotch of one of the aged trees and planted the treasure where a gnarled limb pointed.

With the treasure hidden and all telltale signs carefully removed, the trio began following a path, thinking it might lead them to a settlement. To their delight they soon learned that they were not far from the bayside town of Monterey. With light hearts they made their way into the capital community and headed for the nearest saloon.

As one salute followed another, it was not long before one of the boastful three let the free-flowing whiskey get the best of him. With slurred tongue and bleary eyes he began telling all who would listen of their good fortune. However, before he had a chance to tell the whole story, his two companions jumped him and effectively silenced his boasts.

Unfortunately for the shipwreck survivors, the crowd of Montereyans at the saloon had had their appetites whetted by the tale. As they demanded to hear more about the treasure, a fight broke out, resulting in the death of two of the sailors and the mysterious disappearance of the third. With no one left to reveal the hiding place, several treasure-seeking expeditions failed to find the aged cypress with its gnarled limb pointing the way.

Subsequently, the story was forgotten by all but a few. Years later, however, during the days of whaling at Point Lobos, a lone Indian who worked as a whaler at Whaler's Cove suddenly turned up with a remarkable tale. Having learned of the buried loot, the Indian said, he spent many months in a dedicated search before he found an aged cypress that matched the description of the tree in the tale. Sighting through a crotch in the tree, he saw the remains of a gnarled limb pointing to the ground. He marked the spot and returned late that night with tools in hand.

Carefully, the Indian dug where the limb pointed. Soon the blade of his shovel scraped against something metallic.

With visions of riches welling up in his head, the Indian dropped to his knees to inspect his find. However, just as his fingers groped for the valuables, a mysterious light appeared through the trees from somewhere off the point. Alarmed by the strange and unearthly glow, the frightened Indian wondered whether the ghosts of the shipwreck survivors were watching over their hidden hoard, or whether the spirit of the long-dead ship captain was angry with with him for trying to steal his vessel's wealth. Taking no chances, the would-be treasure seeker frantically began shoveling dirt back into the hole!

With the treasure once again buried, the superstitious Indian left on the run. Never, he vowed, would he return to the treasure site—or tell anyone where he had found the ill-fated fortune.

A lady whose spirit he had been seeking . . .

The Point Lobos area is also the site of a tale of a second shipwreck with a strange and ghostly twist. Although the wreck dates back to the late 1800s, the ghostly events surrounding it were not fully recorded for more than a quarter of a century.

As the story unfolds, several seafarers from turn-of-the-century vessels reported hearing the subdued sounds of a submerged bell as they plied the Pacific off the Point Lobos promontory. Confused by the sounds, coastal travelers speculated whether they might signal the grave of a lost ship, and what the meaning of the sounds could be.

As time went on, reports of the bell-like sounds continued to haunt the men who sailed the treacherous waters off Point Lobos. Finally, the mysterious ringing of the underwater bell became too much for an aged and bewhiskered sea captain, and he hired a diver and crew to attempt to find its source.

Knowing the dangerous, deep-water dives that would ensue, as well as the slim chance of actually finding the bell, the San Francisco-based diver who accepted the job did so only at the insistence of the aged shipmaster—and then only when the price was right. The skipper, who had plotted the locations where he had heard the bell's sounds, supplied a chart and accompanied the diver and crew aboard the diving boat.

With the old skipper looking on, the diver made repeated attempts to find the submerged source of the strange sounds. Finally, while resting at the bottom of the sea on the second day of the search, the diver heard a subdued and distant bell-like sound. Listening intently as he waited in the underwater world of the Pacific, he again heard "a vague wavering tone," almost as if a bell had been struck long before and the ringing sounds were slowly dying in the sea. Following the eerie sounds, he came to a ledge that appeared to "drop forever." Below him, the ringing seemed to fill the sea!

After rising to the surface and reporting his find, as well as the danger that would be involved in making a dive into the depths of the "bottomless canyon," the diver—at the urging of the captain—hesitatingly agreed to make one last dive in a final effort to find the bell and its ship.

Because of the depth of the canyon and the many dangers involved, the diver gave detailed instructions to his crew. He also took special precautions in checking his heavy canvas diving suit and the cumbersome helmet that screwed to its top. Assured that all was right, and with the helmet carefully secured, he signaled that he was ready and pushed himself from the vessel's over-side ladder.

Lowered ever so slowly by the crew, the diver gradually descended into the depths of the Point Lobos chasm. After what seemed an interminable drop, his weighted shoes and groping hands touched a "shadowy something" near the canyon's bottom, and a large seaweed-covered hulk began to emerge beside him. Reaching out in an effort to grasp something solid, the startled diver was surprised at the object's slippery feel. It was then that he realized he had been lowered directly onto a sunken ship!

Concerned about the pressure that exerted itself on his suit—and feeling that he had completed his part of the bargain by finding the vessel from which the mysterious sounds came—the diver signaled the crew to bring him up. As he felt the tug of his lifeline and started toward the surface, he reached out for an object that he could take with him in order to have tangible evidence of his find. On clearing what he thought was the upper works of the vessel, he noticed something jutting toward him at an awkward angle. Grasping the slippery, seaweed-covered object as he went by, he felt it give to his pull, and he carried it with him on his ride to the surface.

After a long and purposely slow ascent, the diver was exhausted when he reached the launch and had to be dragged aboard the boat. As he lay on the deck, too tired to move, concerned crew members hastily unscrewed the helmet's faceplate. With the faceplate and helmet finally removed, and after having been revived by a fresh ocean breeze, the diver saw that the captain was studying the seaweed-covered board that he had brought to the surface.

The barnacle-encrusted and worm-eaten wood proved to be the remains of a ship's nameboard. Together the diver and captain carefully scraped the ocean growth from the rotting wood until they saw the name *Maid of Arden* carved on the board.

When these words appeared, the captain became a changed man. His face took on a peculiar look, and his

15

voice shook with emotion as he announced to the crew that he was going to put on the diving gear and visit the sunken vessel.

Neither the dangers involved nor the emotional pleas of the diver would change the captain's mind. He had paid well for the trip, and he was in sole command. Ignoring the diver's protests, the aged skipper donned the suit and began the dangerous dive.

As the captain's helmet became lost in a flurry of foam and bubbles, the diving boat crew uneasily went about their duties, checking and rechecking the air hose and lifeline. Suddenly, the crew member in charge of the air hose screamed for help as the furiously bubbling line came coiling to the surface unattached! Jumping for the lifeline, the crew hurriedly pulled it to the surface, only to discover that it, too, was unattached. A quick check of the lines revealed the reason—both lines had been cut by the captain! The crew could only stand and watch helplessly, knowing that the boat's skipper would find his final resting place in the depths below.

As word spread up and down the coast of the strange circumstances surrounding the death of the aged shipmaster, the final chapter of the tale began to unfold. As one might guess, the nameboard of the sunken vessel proved to be the key that unlocked the mystery. Upon learning the name of the wrecked ship, a veteran Pacific seafarer who had known the captain offered the information that the *Maid of Arden* had long ago disappeared after setting out from San Francisco on a voyage down the California coast. The seafarer's next comment answered, for many, the question of why the old captain would have chosen to die among the bones of this ship. Aboard the *Maid of Arden* on that fateful last voyage was the skipper's wife, a lady whose spirit he perhaps had been seeking, and who may have beckoned to him through the sounds of a bell . . . summoning him to her side and to the Point Lobos deep where she had long ago died.

Mournful cries from a Highlands hillside . . .

Back on land, and in exploring the southern part of Point Lobos State Reserve, one will come upon China Cove. This tiny inlet and its white sandy beach boasts a colorful history filled with exciting stories about lost treasures, mysterious caves, and long-ago smuggling.

It is the secret trade of smuggling that many believe is the origin of the cove's name. As the story goes, more than a century ago—soon after the introduction of the Chinese Exclusion Bill (1882)—the smuggling of Chinese into secluded seaports along the California coast became a profitable business. Among the landings favored for this purpose by at least one enterprising ship captain was the tiny inlet we know today as China Cove.

South of the cove and of Point Lobos proper is the cliff-clinging community of Carmel Highlands. Among the most captivating of all California's coastal villages, Carmel Highlands—with its dense Pacific fogs, cliff-side homes, and narrow, twisting, tree-lined streets—lends itself to ghostly tales as few communities do.

One of the best known of these stories is an account that is thought to be linked to nearby China Cove and the smuggling of Chinese workers into California. The tragic tale tells of several dozen Chinese workers who were buried alive in a Highlands coal mine. The mine was operated by the Carmelo Land & Coal Company, whose incorporation papers date back to the 1880s, soon after the business of smuggling Chinese went into high gear.

Mining the coal was a complex and dangerous operation. The coal, which is reported to have been of highly gaseous content, was drawn from a lengthy tunnel and 275-foot shaft located to the east of the Carmel Highlands. Despite the difficulties, all went well for members of the coal company during its early years, with plans for a narrow-gauge railroad even being drawn up. However, as time went by several problems arose. Among them was a bunker fire and a ship explosion, the latter taking place at the company's loading facility at nearby Whaler's Cove in Point Lobos. Along with other obstacles that plagued the company, these setbacks resulted in financial problems for the mine's backers.

It is in this context that the reported tragedy involving the Chinese workers occurred. A number of publications have reported that up to seventy Chinese laborers were entombed in the mine. Rumor has it that with a payroll to meet, and little money in the till, the mine's operators herded the workers into the tunnel and then blasted it shut! This simple—if murderous—act conveniently solved the company's payroll problem and did away with the troublesome mine in one operation.

Adding to the credibility of the rumors is information I obtained from an aged member of a pioneer south coast family who is now deceased. When I discussed the mine with him, he matter-of-factly stated that even though the Chinese laborers worked the mine "from dawn till dusk for ten cents a day," the mine's owners were losing money. In his opinion, instead of attempting to pay their help or let them go, the company's operators chose to entomb the workers in the mine's deep shaft.

History buffs have debated for years whether such an "accident" actually occurred and, if so, what may have caused it. As an example, another story that persists to this day agrees there was a cave-in at the mine that took many lives, but maintains it wasn't financial problems that were to blame. This story goes on to tell about a deadly and highly contagious disease (either smallpox or a type of plague) that was being carried by a small number of the mine's workers. Subscribers to this theory believe that, in an attempt to stop the disease from spreading, all of the company's Chinese laborers were herded into the mine, whereupon a healthy plug of dynamite sealed their doom.

The thought of unsuspecting workers being buried alive—whatever the reason may have been—is enough to send shivers down anyone's spine. But there may be more to this story than the mystery of what happened at the mine so many years ago. In 1993 I ran across a fellow who had once worked at the famed Highlands Inn resort. As it turned out, he had read my original Big Sur ghost book and had become fascinated by the Carmel Highlands coal mine.

So, with a fellow worker he hiked to the site. As they stood near the old mine's entrance they began hearing eerie "laughing" sounds that seemed to come from the trees. As the sounds became louder—sounding more and more like they were coming from a man with a high-pitched voice—the pair looked around the area, but could find nothing out of the ordinary. By then my friend's companion (a tall, macho-type individual who weighed about 250 pounds) was so spooked he took off on the run!

Feeling scared himself, but suspecting a prank, my friend bravely took another look around. Although there was no one to be seen, the sounds continued to grow in intensity, and the eerie laugh became more and more demented. Finally, my friend couldn't stand it any longer, and he too hightailed it out of the area!

Today, with no record of how many Chinese were smuggled into China Cove, and no way of knowing whether or not a number of Chinese workers really were buried in the Highlands mine, visitors to the area can only shake their heads in wonder as they marvel at the rusted relics of yesterday and listen to the eerie sounds of the wind as it blows up the canyons and plays in the trees, sounding for all the world like mournful cries coming from some hidden hollow deep within the Highlands hillside . . .

Visitors from the other side . . .

In addition to the long-closed coal mine, a number of haunted houses add to the mystique of Carmel Highlands.

One of these buildings is an elaborate multistoried structure perched high on a hill overlooking the Pacific. Dark and foreboding, this aged building sat vacant for a long period of time and was rumored to be "a refuge for troubled spirits." No doubt, the fact that the dwelling's original owner (and builder) was a rather unique woman who believed in spiritualism and the teachings of Amie Semple McPherson added to the speculation that visitors "from the other side" were responsible for the mysterious goings-on that continued to take place after the owner passed away.

Among these ghostly happenings are doors that mysteriously open and close, lights that turn on and off, and heavy footsteps that have been heard where no living person was known to be. A bit more unusual are the loud thumping noises that have been traced to the building's third story and that may be connected with the sound of footsteps. Because they appear to come from a bedroom, and because they are described as similar to the sounds heavy shoes would make if they were dropped on the floor, more than one visitor has offered the theory that perhaps a long-ago guest had returned to the room, and thoughtfully (if noisily) removed his shoes before stretching out on the bed for a well-deserved rest.

Although the structure's spooky appearance and unexplained happenings are difficult to dismiss, the most unnerving of visitors' experiences are the intense feelings of "not being wanted" that, at times, seem to fill the house. These feelings (or vibrations, as they have often been called) have led several past residents to suggest that the dwelling's original owner still claims the aged building as her own and that she is letting it be known that she continues to crave the privacy she so avidly sought when she was alive. In this connection, it is of interest to note that when the structure was being built, this devotee of spiritualism had a secret passageway installed that enabled her to "disappear at will" and maintain the privacy she desired.

As I describe in my book *Ghost Notes,* in 1979 I spent a couple of hours—in the dark of night—in this mysterious building. Accompanying me were a long-time Carmelite and a retired police officer. As we groped through the darkness, trying to find the front door, the spookiness of the scene was greatly enhanced by the mournful howling of a dog in the distance.

After locating the entrance, we hesitantly explored the three levels of the house by the light of our flashlights, as the electricity was turned off. The house was devoid of furniture, and there was no one, living or otherwise, to be seen. We spent considerable time sitting on the floor in the living room waiting for "the shoe to drop," but all we got for our troubles was a collection of flea bites.

More haunted happenings in Carmel Highlands houses . . .

With our discussion of spiritualism, old houses, and women connected with them, I cannot help but think of Sarah Winchester and the famed Winchester Mystery House of San Jose, California. The 160-room Winchester mansion is perhaps the world's best example of what unlimited funds—and a belief in the occult—can lead to. Tradition states that the widowed Mrs. Winchester was told by a Massachusetts medium that she could gain eternal life, and escape the angry spirits of those killed by the Winchester rifle, if she were to acquire—and continually add to—a West Coast residence. With this as her goal, the diminutive Sarah Winchester traveled to the San Jose area and purchased a farmhouse. So began an odyssey that lasted 38 years, as Sarah spent the rest of her life creating the bizarre—and hauntingly beautiful—Winchester mansion as her spirit friends directed.

Although it is thought that the closest Sarah Winchester ever got to Carmel Highlands was Monterey's magnificent Hotel Del Monte, there are those who believe her influence definitely reached this coastal community. Evidence of this is an elaborate hillside house that boasts a history of constantly being added to. Even though it is not nearly as large as the Winchester mansion, legend states that the woman of the house was under the impression that as long as she kept building, she would never die. The result is an elaborate edifice containing, among many other things, seven bedrooms, all elegantly appointed and all with fireplaces (the largest of which was big enough for a man to walk into).

Also on the grounds of this stately structure is a detached library building. Like the main house, this structure is said to be haunted. Behind locked doors the distinct sounds of the building's first owner—who has been dead for many years—have repeatedly been heard as she pleads with the butler to let her leave.

A second haunted Carmel Highlands house also boasts "a voice from the past." The man who told me this tale introduced himself as "the head of the house." The voice he described had been heard by several people, and it frequently joined in conversation with two members of his family. Whose voice it was, or why it was so selective about whose conversation it joined, no one seems to know.

While I found this story of interest, I soon learned that the teller of this tale was just getting warmed up. Not only did his next account make quite an impression on me, but from the tone of his voice and the look on his face, I could see that it had also made quite an impression on *him* (in fact, it almost made an impression *of* him in the wall of his house!).

The man shook his head in wonder as he began his story. As he described it, he was in the large living room of his "Highlands hacienda" when he suddenly realized that the baby grand piano had started to move. As he stared in awe, the instrument began to pick up speed and head straight for him! Dumbfounded, he watched in horror as the piano raced toward him and then—just as it was about to smash him into the wall—suddenly came to a stop, leaving him barely enough room to escape!

It was the next series of happenings, however, that proved to be the clincher and convinced him it was time to move. On two occasions, he said, his daughter woke up in hysterics. Upon hearing her frantic screams, the entire household rushed to her room. There they found a rat that appeared to be drugged lying on her bed near her head!

The man concluded his stories by saying that since their move he has kept an eye on the house. To no one's surprise who is aware of his family's experiences, the building has been vacant more often than not!

Trouble at Bad Crossing Creek . . .

Long before automobiles became commonplace, when the vision of a coast highway was still only a dream, there was a wagon road that led south of Carmel Highlands and toward the primitive paradise of Big Sur. Winding through canyons and along rocky cliffs, this long-ago coast route was beautiful to look at—as long as one had plenty of time, and the winter rains and summer fogs hadn't set in—but torturous to travel.

Slightly south of the Highlands a small stream flows from the rugged Santa Lucia Mountains and meets the Pacific in a mass of bubbly foam. According to old-timers, this mountain stream was aptly named Mal Paso Creek (meaning "bad crossing" or "difficult passage"). Those who were forced to travel the coast trail would shake their heads in anguish and tell of being stranded in the muddy bottom of "Bad Crossing Creek" for as long as a day.

Near this crossing an event took place that has become a part of local lore. As the story goes, long ago a wagon driver was hauling a load of tanbark (used for the tanning of hides) out of the Santa Lucias. The man followed a steep and narrow trail that clung to a Mal Paso Canyon cliff. In the distance he could see that the trail made a sharp bend as it followed the mountain stream near the canyon's bottom.

Concerned about the bend and the steep incline that preceded it, the driver set the brakes on his wagon and carefully checked his team and his load of tanbark. With everything seemingly in order, he started down the trail.

The bells on the collar of the lead horse jangled monotonously as the team cautiously made its way down the incline. Suddenly, the brakes on the heavily loaded wagon gave out. Unable to hold it back, the driver stayed with his rig, struggling to keep both the team and the wagon on the trail. However, when they came to the sharp bend near the canyon's bottom, the wagon was going much too fast to round the curve. The frightened four-horse team—along with the driver and his load of tanbark—plunged over the side and into the creek below.

As the story ends, the driver is said to have been killed, while the tanbark was strewn up and down the canyon floor. As to the fate of the horses, no mention is made.

What gives this tale its ghostly flavor is the comment that concludes this long-ago account: "For a number of years after the accident people who used the trail at night swore they could hear the bells of the lead horse as they passed the spot where the wagon went over the side!"

The invisible wagon was always headed west . . .

The preceding tale is only one of several Santa Lucia stories about bells and runaway wagons. A number of these accounts take place in the areas of Mal Paso Creek and

Palo Colorado Canyon, approximately six miles to the south, and some of them show marked similarities. I'll recount two of these tales here.

The first story comes from an old-timer who was reminiscing about some of the things he remembered most about living on the Big Sur coast in the early 1930s, including the building of the highway (which celebrated its grand opening in 1937). One of his accounts told about how, as a lad, he would take his rifle into the Santa Lucia Mountains to hunt for rabbits. As he explored the foothills, he often heard the distinct, but distant, sound of bells.

Confused about the source of the sounds, he finally asked his dad about them. Indicating that he too had heard the bells, his father explained that, according to legend, many years before a stage driver on the Big Sur run attached bells to his coach so people could hear him coming from a long distance away. One day—when his rig was high-balling down a grade—something spooked the horses, causing the driver to lose control of his team. Upon rounding a bend at breakneck speed, the coach took a tumble, killing the driver (does this sound familiar?). As the story ends, the bells that are frequently heard throughout the foothills are the sounds of the stagecoach as it continues to make its ghostly run.

The second tale involves an incident that took place in Palo Colorado Canyon. Various publications say that Palo Colorado means "redwood," "red stick," or "red mast." In any case, most locals agree that the canyon gained its name from its many redwood trees. These trees are important to our story, which involves a small settlement that once stood on a flat near the canyon's entrance. Bordering the Pacific, the tiny town was founded by William and Godfrey Notley, and was known throughout the area as Notley's Landing.

The Notley brothers operated a mill in the canyon and presided over a small lumber empire. With the help of many workers they felled trees, sawed lumber, and cut quantities of shakes, shingles, railroad ties, and posts. This wood, along with a substantial amount of tanbark, was brought to the mouth of the canyon by various means, including cable, sleds, the backs of mules, and heavy-duty lumber wagons. When the wood reached the flat, it was loaded on small coastal freighters and lumber schooners that periodically called at the landing.

After the lumber mill shut down (with much of its equipment being moved to another Big Sur location), the small town, along with "the wildest dance hall on the south coast," gradually disappeared. Incidentally, this "dog-hole shipping port," as the landing was sometimes called, is also rumored to have been the site of Chinese smuggling, and, during the Prohibition years of the 1920s, rum-running.

With this background, let's get to the story of the run-away wagon. Long ago, it is said, when workers and residents of the Palo Colorado area were in the habit of walking down the canyon road at night, they often heard the sounds of a spirited team and a wild-riding wagon charging down the trail behind them. Diving for shelter, or hiding behind a nearby tree, they would peer into the inky black of the Palo Colorado night, hoping to catch a glimpse of the thundering steeds and the hard-charging wagon. However, the sounds of the pounding hoof-beats and the clatter of the wagon's wheels always passed them by without anyone ever seeing the source of the sounds!

Who owned the wagon? Where was it going? Was there a driver spurring the horses on? No one knows. All any-one can say is that the invisible team and wagon were always headed west and that, wherever they were going, they were in a terrible hurry!

Now, as to whether there is a connection between the last three stories, as some have suggested, your guess is as good as mine. Perhaps in their many retellings over the years, the accounts—and their locations—have been changed. Whatever the source of the tales may be, they continue to endure in local lore—as does the fact that no hoofprints or wagon tracks have ever been found at any of the sites.

Two letters trimmed in black . . .

Interestingly, the sounds of bells are a prominent part of yet another tale that takes place in the Mal Paso Creek/Palo Colorado Canyon area. This story has become one of my favorite Big Sur coast accounts. In this case, however, the bells are not connected with wagons, stagecoaches, or invisible teams of horses. Instead, they are the bells of an aged church located halfway around the world.

I heard this account many years ago from a man in his eighties who has long since died. He had lived much of his life on a seaside ranch between Mal Paso Creek and Palo Colorado Canyon. It was here that the incident took place, and the person who experienced it was a close friend of the man who told me the tale.

Occurring approximately 100 years ago, the event—and the circumstances surrounding it—were the talk of the Big Sur coast in the early 1900s. The story involves a man of Portuguese descent who had only recently arrived in this country from the Azores (a group of islands about 800 miles off the coast of Portugal). Working as a ranch hand, the man was given Sundays off to do as he pleased. Loving horses, and the Santa Lucias, he would often take long horseback rides into the coastal mountains on his day off.

Late one Sunday, after riding for hours in the Santa Lucias, the worker was heading back to the ranch headquarters when he came upon a small canyon with a stream flowing through it. Being tired from his ride, and knowing his horse was thirsty, he let the animal drink while he lay in the tall grass watching the clouds drift in from the Pacific. It was while he was watching the clouds, and feeling at peace with himself and his surroundings, that he heard the sounds of tolling church bells.

Surprised by the sounds, the man listened intently. He was even more surprised when he realized that the bells sounded exactly like those in his distant island church. Confused as to how he could hear his village bells in a mountain canyon thousands of miles from his home, he mounted his horse and rode to the main house, where he told his story.

Interested in the tale, but not taking it seriously, the owners of the ranch (as well as others who heard about the incident) were of the opinion that the ranch hand had drifted off to sleep in the peaceful surroundings of the mountain canyon and had simply dreamed that he had heard the mournful tolling of bells.

Convinced he had not been dreaming, and that the sounds were very real, the ranch hand returned to the canyon at about the same time of day on the following Sunday. As he had done the week before, he let his horse drink while he lay down to rest. Once again he heard the distinct sounds of the bells of his village church! Positive he wasn't dreaming, he again mounted his horse and raced to the ranch house, where he repeated his story.

Discussing the event much more seriously on this second occasion, the people of the ranch began to wonder whether someone from the worker's distant village was trying to contact him. Perhaps, they suggested, something had happened to a member of his family. With no way to communicate with California—except by extremely slow ship-going mail—perhaps others in the family were trying to inform him of the situation through the ringing of the church bells.

The next week, the ranch hand again visited the canyon. To his relief, there were no sounds of church bells to be heard. When an additional week passed without the sounds of bells, the event was gradually forgotten, and things went back to normal.

It wasn't until approximately six weeks after the worker had first heard the bells of his faraway church that the matter again became very real to the people of the Big Sur coast. On that fateful day, the ranch hand received two letters trimmed in black. Upon opening the letters, he immediately realized the significance of the bells. Exactly one week apart—on the very days he had heard the bells—his mother and his father had died in his far-off village in the Azores!

He was certain *something* was there . . .

Not far from the canyon of the tolling church bells a second odd event took place. This incident occurred in the 1930s and indirectly involves the work of the acclaimed poet Robinson Jeffers. As most literary folk know, Jeffers lived in Carmel most of his life, and much of his work was inspired by the rugged beauty of the Big Sur coast.

The story concerns a Monterey Peninsula photographer who was taking pictures of selected locations along the coast that Jeffers had written about. The photos were to be used to illustrate one of the poet's many books. It was hoped that the pictures would help the reader appreciate both the verse and the grandeur of this wilderness region.

One gray day the photographer drove south on Highway One past Monastery Beach, Point Lobos, and the Carmel Highlands. Shortly after crossing the Mal Paso Creek bridge, he pulled to a stop. Gathering his equipment, he made his way through the morning fog and started up a nearby hill. Birds chirped and cows grazed as he trudged through the wet grass. However, as he climbed above the fog and gazed out over a sea of white, all sounds suddenly ceased. Feeling uncomfortable in the eerie silence—almost as if he was being watched—he nevertheless continued up the slope. Soon he reached the top of the hill and the rock formation he wanted to photograph. Glancing around to be sure he was alone, he hurriedly set up his camera and tripod.

When everything was ready, the photographer ducked under the black camera cloth to take his first picture. By then, the uncomfortable feeling of being watched was so intense that each time he slipped under the cloth he sensed a presence on the hill with him. But, whenever he peeked out to see who—or what—was there, there was never anything to be seen. Still, the longer he stayed on the hill the more uncomfortable he became. Finally, he couldn't stand it any longer. Quickly gathering his equipment, he made a beeline for his car. What had caused the feelings he couldn't say, but he was certain *something* was there!

Later he shared his experience with Jeffers' wife, Una. She showed little surprise and casually indicated that he had merely been in the presence of the "little people."

Now, just who the "little people" are, I'm not sure. However, the photographer's tale and Una's remark remind me that mysterious beings have long been said to inhabit the Santa Lucias. These creatures, whatever they may be, have been a part of Big Sur lore for as long as anyone can remember. We will encounter them a little later in this book (see "The dark watchers of the Santa Lucias . . . ," page 48).

The Palo Colorado miss with the long golden hair . . .

Before leaving the lovely Mal Paso Creek/Palo Colorado Canyon areas behind, I'd like to touch on at least one more tale about this region. The problem is that there are several stories from which to choose, each with its own unanswered questions and unique mystique. The "ghost boat," nestled high on a Palo Colorado hill and practically hidden from view by second-growth timber and dense foliage, is one example. And then there are the ghostly remains of a World War II bomber—complete with an odd assortment of bones—that were found on the slopes of a nearby peak in 1973. (In case you're wondering, yes, the bomber *was* one of ours!)

But perhaps it would be best to get back to a more traditional kind of ghost story. With this in mind, I'd like to share an account about the ghostly figure of a pretty young lass whose image has often been seen along the banks of the creek that runs through Palo Colorado Canyon.

I was introduced to this story by a pair of long-time Monterey Peninsulans who are now deceased. They learned it from a pioneer south coast family that proudly traces its Palo Colorado heritage back to the 1800s. According to their account, many years ago (perhaps more than 100) an attractive young lady who lived in the canyon was tragically killed—whether in an accident or by foul play, they could not say. Not long after her untimely death, residents of the canyon reported seeing her image on moonlit nights along the banks of the creek near the site where she died. As described by numerous people over a period of many years, the long-ago lass always appeared to be happy, and she was always observed combing her long hair. This detail perhaps makes sense when we consider the rumors that she was on her way to meet her lover when she was killed. With this in mind, the old-timers speculated that the ghostly miss might have been using the light of the moon to see her reflection in one of the stream's pools.

The young lady's image continued to be seen for many years, with the last report I know of coming from the latter half of the 1900s. In fact, I recently ran into a Big Sur resident who claimed to have seen the "ghostly girl" when she was a young lady herself.

31

One old-timer's comment provides a fitting end to this tale. As this long-time resident of the area remarked, "If combing her locks kept the lass happy and helped ease her pain, it's a fine way to remember the Palo Colorado miss with the long golden hair."

The glowing figure reminded him of an "old wizard" . . .

Our next story comes from a man who was a witness to the event he described. Although my informer couldn't pinpoint the exact spot on the coast highway where this incident occurred, on the basis of his description I am of the opinion that it took place slightly to the south of Palo Colorado Canyon.

I learned about this incident late one March evening in 1999 when I received a call from a man in southern California whom I will call Frank. The caller asked if I was the fellow who wrote the book *Incredible Ghosts of the Big Sur Coast*. After I acknowledged that I was, Frank began telling me about an odd event he had experienced in the Big Sur area approximately ten years before.

The happening occurred when he and a friend were driving north on Highway One, heading for the Monterey Peninsula. At about ten o'clock at night, when they were still many miles from Carmel, they saw a mysterious white light in the road ahead of them. At first glance they thought it was a car coming toward them. But as they got closer, it became obvious that the light was not coming from a car.

When they drew abreast of the light, they were astonished to see a man with a long white beard walking beside the road. He was dressed in a light-colored robe, "similar to a monk's habit," and he was holding a staff, "like a shepherd's, complete with a hook at its end." His hair was also long and white, and he had sandals on his feet.

"Strangest of all," continued Frank (who was in the passenger seat and was in awe of what was going on), a strange white light seemed to emerge from the figure, "almost as if it glowed in the dark." Frank compared the man's appearance to that of an old wizard, saying that he was reminded of "Merlin the magician." As they passed the lonely figure, Frank turned and watched in wonder as it "continued to glow" until their car rounded a bend and it was lost from sight.

Even though Frank often wondered about what he and his partner had seen that night, he chose not to share his experience with many people because of the raised eyebrows and looks of disdain he would receive upon telling his story. Recently, however, he had seen a television program involving a ghost from the Chicago area that "glowed." Reminded of his Big Sur coast experience, he started making phone calls and visiting bookstores that specialized in "weird things." He also browsed the Internet, where he learned of my Big Sur ghost book. After ordering a copy, and failing to see any accounts about wizard-like men who glowed in the dark, he called me to find out if I had heard any such stories since the book was published.

I could only tell Frank that the apparition in his account was new to me and that I couldn't answer his question of who the man might be. Who knows, maybe he was a holdover from the 1960s, when Big Sur was a magnet for counterculture types. After all, one of the great gurus of that time once holed up in a cabin not far from where Frank saw the "wizard," and at a later date—in one frantic ten-day binge—he cranked out a book that immortalized the area to those of his kind. The book, of course, was *Big Sur*, and its author was none other than Jack Kerouac, the father of the Beat Generation.

So perhaps Frank's "wizard" was one of the Beats, making a pilgrimage to a time that was. Of course, that doesn't explain why the old man glowed . . .

A ghostly airplane of World War I vintage . . .

Down the road and around a few bends from where the "wizard" sighting probably took place, one comes to the canyon where Jack Kerouac holed up. Famous to television viewers for the fabulous Bixby Creek Bridge that crosses it (and for the countless commercials that have been filmed there), the canyon and its bridge are among the Big Sur region's most talked-about attractions. Considered the "engineering triumph" of the coast road, Bixby Bridge was completed in 1932. Originally known as Rainbow Bridge, it has been described as one of the world's highest single-span concrete arch bridges. It is little wonder that it draws people from far and near to marvel at its construction and gaze at the surrounding vistas. For many locals and visitors alike, the bridge has always been one of the highlights of the Big Sur coast.

A fascinating footnote to the history of the bridge concerns an event that occurred the day after the official opening of the Carmel-to-Cambria coast highway in 1937. Al Geer, a local resident and pilot, decided to try flying a plane *under* the bridge's graceful arch! Approaching the bridge from the landward side, he zoomed beneath the span and out over the water. As the *Monterey Herald* commented in 1987, "In a peculiar way, Geer's feat symbolizes construction of the highway: it seemed an impossible task, but it was done and the result was spectacular."

Long before the Bixby Bridge was even a dream, however, the Monterey Lime Company (of Bixby Canyon) also drew visitors from far and near. Those long-ago tourists came to view an aerial tramway that transported enormous buckets of lime down the rugged canyon to Bixby Point, where it was loaded aboard small coastal freighters. Unfortunately, this turn-of-the-century company did not survive for long, and along with the community that

34

The Carmelite Monastery as it appeared about the time it was completed (1931). The facility is located along the banks of San Jose Creek and across Highway One from Monastery Beach. For purposes of this publication, the Big Sur coast begins in the vicinity of San Jose Creek, as do the stories in this book.

Point Lobos State Reserve boasts one of the Big Sur coast's most colorful histories. Shown above is part of this picturesque promontory. The entrance to Whaler's Cove is visible to the left. Inset shows the Veteran Cypress, a gnarled and aged Point Lobos tree. As discussed in the text, perhaps the earthbound roots of this tree contain the entrapped souls of a forgotten race.

Located near the mouth of Palo Colorado Canyon was the coastal community of Notley's Landing. Among other distinctions, this long-gone settlement boasted the "wildest dance hall" on the Monterey County coast. Inset shows the precarious position of some of the buildings.

Almost hidden by the foliage of Palo Colorado Canyon are the ghostly re-mains of a long-ago lumber mill. A close look at this neglected equipment brings to mind a time that was.

The Monterey Lime Company played an important part in the early history of Bixby Canyon. About all that is left of this colorful period are the kilns' ghostly chimneys that point toward the sky. Inset shows a portion of the aerial tramway that transported buckets of lime to Bixby Point.

On the edge of Bixby Point were several Monterey Lime Company buildings. This was also the terminus of the aerial tramway. On the Bixby Point cliff was a somewhat rickety-appearing chute (inset), where barrels of lime were loaded aboard small coastal freighters.

The building of the coast road was a magnificent feat, with the construction of Bixby Creek Bridge considered by many to have been the crowning achievement of the entire project. Although there are many accounts about the bridge and the canyon that it crosses, perhaps the most talked-about tale is the story of a ghostly airplane of World War I vintage that flies under the bridge's gracefully curving arch (inset). People still talk about hearing the airplane as it flies under the bridge and up the narrow canyon (as depicted in the cover art for this book).

While not ghostly, the wreck of the U.S.S. *Macon* is an important part of Big Sur history. An incredible aircraft in every respect, the loss of this "silver lady" was not only a blow to the United States Navy, but to lighter-than-air buffs throughout the world. Being 785 feet long, and containing four Curtiss Sparrowhawk airplanes in her hull, the giant dirigible was lost off Point Sur on February 12, 1935. Inset shows the 3,000-ton coastal freighter *Babinda* before her phantom skipper and ghostly crew guided the fire-ravaged vessel to her final resting place in Point Sur's Pacific graveyard of ships.

Point Sur and its lighthouse are familiar landmarks to travelers of Highway One as well as to seafarers along the Big Sur coast. Claiming numerous vessels over the years, the waters around this Pacific promontory contain the remains of the *Macon* and *Babinda*, as well as the "twin shipwrecks" of the *Ventura* and *Los Angeles*. Inset shows several structures atop Point Sur rock, including the lightkeeper's house (with chimneys) that is haunted by a teenage girl.

Considered a sacred mountain by certain Indians of the Monterey County coast, Pico Blanco (White Mountain or Peak) may also hold the secret of Al Clark's "underground world."

The cabin of Alfred K. Clark as it appeared in the early 1930s. It was near this cabin that Clark (inset) discovered the Silver King Mine and Big Sur's subterranean world of "elephants with long shaggy hair" and "cats with long sharp teeth."

The Post house, circa 1860s, is one of the Sur's oldest and most recognizable buildings. It is located approximately three miles south of the entrance to Pfeiffer Big Sur State Park and at one time was the "end of the line" for folks traveling down the old coast road. Other than a ghost, this landmark dwelling once housed the Big Sur post office.

Long before man scarred the landscape with dynamite and dump trucks, the Big Sur coast was a primitive and peaceful paradise. Perhaps it was during this time that the Santa Lucia's mysterious dark watchers surveyed the scene with satisfaction rather than fears of overpopulation and pollution.

Among the many mysteries that surround the Los Burros Mining District are the human bones that were found at Massacre Cave.

42

A true ghost of the past is the mining community of Manchester. Known as "The Lost City of the Santa Lucias," this mountain town of yesterday was the hub of Monterey County's remote Los Burros Mining District, and its site is not far from the Ghost of Gold claim.

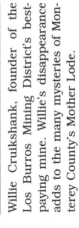

Willie Cruikshank, founder of the Los Burros Mining District's best-paying mine. Willie's disappearance adds to the many mysteries of Monterey County's Mother Lode.

The Gem Saloon was among the favorite gathering places for the people of the mining community of Manchester.

supported it, soon became little more than memories. Among the modern-day relics of this bygone era are huge chimneys from aged lime kilns that rise from a forest of poison oak and chaparral. Reaching for the sky, these gaunt survivors of yesteryear remind passers-by of a long-ago time when Bixby Canyon was alive with people rather than neglected ghosts of the past.

Ghostly tales of a different kind that are connected with Bixby Canyon can perhaps be traced to the tragedy of a construction worker who is said to have fallen into the concrete pour during the building of the bridge's north column, or to the five restaurant workers who lost their lives during a 1948 "massacre" along the canyon's north rim.

On a less grisly note, the Bixby tale that tops them all is the story of a ghostly airplane of World War I vintage that has been observed approaching the canyon from the sea. As if seeing the ghostly image of an aged biplane zeroing in on Bixby Bridge isn't enough to unnerve one on its own, the pilot of this antique craft reverses Al Geer's 1937 feat by flying under the bridge and up the canyon!

To this day, there are those who claim to hear the sounds of the biplane echoing off the canyon walls. One can only wonder who the "spirited" pilot is, and why he repeatedly engages in this daring display of fearless flying.

Bathed in the glow of a halo-like luminescence . . .

Since we're on the subject of odd aircraft along the Big Sur coast, I think the following tale—even though it strays a bit from the subject of ghosts—is appropriate at this point.

Reported to have taken place in the 1950s, the event, although not common knowledge at the time, is said to have created quite a stir among those who were aware of it. The incident occurred one dark night when a teenage couple was parked along a narrow and lonely coast road. The road, which was private, unpaved, and seldom used, led off of Highway One and into the Santa Lucias. After finding a suitable place to stop, the couple parked for a period of time. Suddenly the darkness of the night and the peacefulness of the scene were shattered by an incredibly bright light! Staring in shocked silence, the teenagers saw a huge, circular object hovering over the area they had recently driven through. Terrified by the sight, and being only a few hundred yards from the light source, the couple watched in wide-eyed wonder as the low-flying craft's unearthly light lit up the landscape as if it were day.

As it happens, the boy was a photography student at a local high school, and he faithfully carried his equipment with him. After the initial shock of seeing the strange object began to lessen, he grabbed his camera and he and his partner cautiously crept from the car. With a hush in the air and not a breath of wind stirring, the teenagers took pains not to break the unnatural silence. As the enormous object and its brilliant "crown of light" continued to hover, the frightened lad took several pictures of the strange craft.

Suddenly, completely without warning and at a speed faster than the eye could follow, the mystery craft "shot" to a spot directly above the shaken couple! Bathed in the glow of a halo-like luminescence, the teenagers clung to each other and shielded their eyes from the blinding light. Too scared to cry, and knowing it was useless to run, the couple huddled together and awaited their fate.

After what seemed like an eternity, the huge craft and its eerie light disappeared from view as quickly and quietly as they had originally appeared. Not waiting for an encore, the thankful couple jumped into their car and raced from the scene.

The following day the boy took his camera to school and, in the privacy of the high school's darkroom, he developed the film. Elated by the quality of the pictures, and the brilliance with which the mysterious ring of light appeared, he proudly showed the film to his instructor. Amazed by the images, and concerned as to what they might be, the photography teacher wasted little time in notifying authorities. With amazing rapidity the film was confiscated, never to be seen again by the boy or his instructor!

As I write this account, it is unknown where the film is or what type of craft (or illusion) made the strange light. What is known, or at least what is still talked about by those in the know, is that a second—and perhaps related—mystery exists to this day as to what burned a huge circular imprint on the grass of a large clearing not far from where the couple spotted the aircraft! Discovered not long after the sighting took place, the round marking adds much to the drama and can only make one wonder what kind of an object it was that touched down in the Santa Lucia wilderness, and what strange creatures may have exited from its hold.

Although it may be tempting to dismiss this tale as a wild dream of UFO enthusiasts, adding credence to the story is the fact that over the years several mysterious objects have been reported in the vicinity of the Big Sur coast. One brief account from a 1950 issue of the *Monterey Peninsula Herald* serves as proof to many that documentation of such sightings does exist. According to the article, a Monterey woman saw "a brilliantly lighted object . . . streaking over the ocean . . . off Carmel Highlands." Further, a lady from the town of Chualar (east of the Santa Lucia Mountains), told of an object that "swooped down" over her car, giving off "a strange bluish-white light that hurt our eyes like a welder's torch." With this account fitting nicely with what the teen photographer and his companion described, and with more than one person having been in the car to witness the event, one can only wonder whether the mysterious objects in these reports were, in fact, one and the same . . . and, if so, exactly what it was that visited this corner of the Earth a half-century ago and left its calling card in the mountains of Big Sur in the form of a singed ring of grass.

The dark watchers of the Santa Lucias . . .

The interesting story of a strange, and possibly unearthly, aircraft touching down on a coastal mountain flat brings to mind the Santa Lucias' mysterious "dark watchers" (mentioned in "He was certain *something* was there . . . ," page 29). Rumors of the existence of such creatures are familiar to historians and pioneer settlers of the Big Sur coast, and have stirred up considerable controversy among many of the area's aged residents for many years.

Adding spice—and credence—to the stories of the "watchers" is the fact that two of Monterey County's literary greats—both of whom knew the coastal mountains well—seem to have included references to them in their works. John Steinbeck, born in the nearby community of Salinas, and winner of the Nobel and Pulitzer Prizes for literature, told of the dark watchers in his short story "Flight." In the story, a character sees "a black figure" on a barren spur and looks quickly away, "for it was one of the dark watchers." Steinbeck continues, "No one knew who the watchers were, nor where they lived, but it was better to ignore them and never to show interest in them." Even more mysteriously, the famed poet Robinson Jeffers wrote in his poem "Such Counsels You Gave to Me" of "forms that look human to human eyes, but certainly are not human. They come from behind ridges and watch."

These descriptions, both of which were published in the 1930s—the same decade that the photographer I described earlier felt an unexplained presence—helped focus attention on the Big Sur country's mysterious dark watchers and the puzzling question of the identity of these "human-like" forms. As would be expected, with the fame of these authors spreading worldwide, visitors from distant shores came to see for themselves, and to this day people keep a sharp eye open for the "silent sentinels" of the Santa Lucias.

Admittedly, these references in the works of Steinbeck and Jeffers are brief and open to interpretation. However, there is no doubt that tales of the dark watchers have been in circulation for decades. In fact, Steinbeck's mother, while teaching school at Big Sur in the late 1800s, reported seeing "dark" people who stood about three feet high. Supposedly, these beings were most often observed "clustered against the canyon walls and in the depths of the redwood forests." Author Rosalind Sharpe Wall, who grew up along the Big Sur coast, also reported seeing what she termed "little dark people," adding that this was "long before I ever heard of them from Robinson Jeffers." In her book *When the Coast Was Wild and Lonely,* Wall also relates that Ed "Doc" Ricketts, the friend of John Steinbeck memorialized in *Cannery Row,* told her of seeing the "little dark people." Furthermore, she was sure that Steinbeck himself believed in them.

With these persistent stories of mysterious watchers on my mind, I cannot help but wonder about the possibility of a connection with the reported sightings of otherworldly craft in the Santa Lucias. If a vehicle of other than earthly origin really did leave a singed ring of grass as a calling card in the mountains of Big Sur, how many other such visitations—perhaps going back hundreds of years—might have taken place unobserved? Are there additional mementos deep within the heart of the Santa Lucias, in areas that perhaps have not been fully explored since the long-ago days of the California Indians? And are there beings who, to this day, roam the mountains and valleys of the Santa Lucias guarding mysterious secrets of their own?

The faceless figure stared at him through eyeless sockets . . .

With John Steinbeck and Robinson Jeffers having alluded to the Santa Lucias' dark watchers in the 1930s, and tales of peculiar creatures having been part of Big Sur lore for many years before that, you may wonder whether stories of mysterious sightings in the area are only "ancient history." In fact, I know of two reports that bring us to considerably more recent times.

The first account was related by a prominent Monterey Peninsula man who was the principal of a local high school. In the mid 1960s, this man, in the company of two friends, was on a hunting trip in the rugged coastal mountains. After much hiking he became separated from his companions but was able to keep them in sight, as they were on a parallel ridge some distance away. As he continued up the hill he was climbing, he frequently glanced at his friends, not wanting to lose them in the wilderness. Suddenly, as he looked toward the opposite ridge, he noticed a strange dark figure standing on a ledge between him and the hill his companions were on.

Quietly, the principal studied the lonely figure. He later described it as being dressed all in black, complete with a cape (or long coat) and hat.

The dark figure stood like a statue as it surveyed the rugged mountain landscape. But when the principal shouted to his friends to turn around and look, the mysterious figure instantly vanished.

In itself, this story might not give us pause, but in the context of the scores of other tales of mysterious "watchers" in the Santa Lucias, one can only wonder just what the principal saw that day.

Even more striking is the second account, which involved another prominent Monterey Peninsula man, in this case a policeman. The year was 1975, and the policeman was out hunting in the coastal mountains.

Suddenly, while he was hiking in a remote area, he saw what appeared to be a "faceless" figure staring at him uncannily through "eyeless sockets." The stare was so intense that it seemed to pass right through him and "peer off into the distance." Much of the figure's face was covered, "as if by a bandanna." Its body was cloaked in a black cape or poncho, and it had a hat or hood covering most of its head. The policeman glanced down at his rifle to cock it, but when he looked up again, the figure had vanished!

Much like the principal, the policeman told this story in sober seriousness. Although accounts such as these leave us with more questions than answers, they make it harder to dismiss the age-old tales of dark watchers in the rugged wilderness of the Santa Lucias.

Albino fish, mastodons, and saber-toothed tigers . . .

In following cliff-clinging Highway One south of Bixby Canyon and around Hurricane Point (where the wind never seems to cease), one comes to a small valley with a river running through it. The Spanish called the stream El Rio Chiquito del Sur, the Little River of the South. Up the winding stream toward the coastal mountains is one of my favorite Santa Lucia locations and the site of our next story.

To appreciate this tale, and the area in which it takes place, we must go back to the days of the dons, perhaps to the time they bestowed the name upon the river. According to aged accounts, more than two centuries ago the Spanish obtained wire silver from the Little Sur Indians. With this setting the scene, we now move ahead to the latter 1800s. It was during this period that Civil War veteran Alfred K. Clark—who came west after the war and homesteaded in the Little Sur area—befriended the last surviving member of the Little Sur Indians. With none of his people left to pass his stories on to, and in gratitude for being taken care of during his dying days, the Indian told Clark about the silver and where it was located. As it happens, the location was in the vicinity of the Civil War veteran's homestead.

After the Indian died, Clark wasted little time in seeking the mine's source. This search—and what he discovered—consumed the rest of his life, in the process turning Clark into a recluse, and a living legend of the Sur.

In his quest for silver, Clark discovered a treasure of another kind, one that remains unexplained to this day. In a scene that recalls how he learned of the mine's location, Clark waited until he was on his deathbed before he divulged his secret, and even then he told only his most trusted friends. Seemingly delirious, Clark told of breaking into a huge natural cavern while working to extend the mine's tunnel. Upon exploring this immense underground opening, he discovered a second and third chamber, as well as a subterranean river, albino fish, cone-like rock formations that resembled icicles, sparkling walls, Indian mortars, and, most amazing of all, ghostly likenesses of "elephants with long shaggy hair" and "cats with long sharp teeth."

Even though many of Clark's claims sounded far-fetched—even to those who were at his side—most of them have plausible scientific explanations. The chambers or underground caverns were, quite possibly, natural formations of limestone. This type of rock is found in abundance in certain sections of the Little Sur. In fact, Pico Blanco (White Peak or Mountain), which is located in the area of the mine—and which towers above the Little Sur River and can easily be seen from Highway One—contains the highest quality of dolomite limestone on the central California coast. Limestone lends itself to "icicle" as well as cone-like rock formations, which are commonly called stalactites and stalagmites. Subterranean rivers are also known to exist in limestone formations and, to make things of even more interest, the south fork of the Little Sur River is said to flow underground in the vicinity of the mine.

As to Clark's "albino fish," creatures of this sort are sometimes found in underground rivers. Referred to as troglobites (cave dwellers), these odd fish lose their eyesight and body pigment due to the length of time they have lived in darkness. The sparkling walls that Clark mentioned could have been the natural cave or cavern walls that contained flakes from a variety of reflective minerals. The mortars—to many—mean that at some long-ago time there was a natural entrance to this "underground world" (an entrance that may still exist), and that people of a past age worked or lived in the vast chambers.

Certainly of most interest, and without doubt the most important of Clark's discoveries, are the wall paintings of strange elephant and cat-like creatures. These paintings were obviously meant to depict the mammoth or mastodon and the saber-toothed tiger. Creatures such as these are known to have roamed the California wilderness long ago. The catch is, that was before humans are thought to have arrived in this area!

One can only wonder what forgotten race of people once lived along the Big Sur coast, frequented a huge underground cavern, and painted pictures of creatures that no longer exist. Those who wish to speculate further about the meaning of this tale may be interested in knowing that—according to the mythology of certain Indians who lived along the Monterey County coast—the Little Sur's magnificent Pico Blanco was a sacred mountain . . . a mountain where the human race had its beginning.

Hmm, could there be a dark watcher connection here? Did "little people" inhabit the cavern? Or did human beings roam the wilderness with giant creatures of the past? Could voyagers from a mysterious space vehicle help solve the puzzle?

Commanded by a phantom skipper and manned by a ghostly crew . . .

Among the colorful accounts connected with the history of Big Sur are the many stories of shipwrecks that have taken place off the Point Sur promontory. Point Sur is a giant rock that rises from the water (and beach) a couple of miles south of the Little Sur River. A lighthouse was built on it in 1889, and, as you will learn in the next section, the lightkeeper's house is haunted by a lady ghost (as is the Point Pinos lighthouse on the Monterey Peninsula).

The waters off Point Sur must also have their share of ghosts when you consider the number of ships that have met tragic ends there. In fact, this rugged stretch of coast has claimed so many vessels that it is sometimes referred to as Big Sur's Pacific graveyard of ships.

In 1935, the Point's watery graveyard became the final resting place of the largest ship ever to have been lost along the coast. But this craft did not float on water. Instead, it was an airship known as the U.S.S. *Macon*. The last of Uncle Sam's super dirigibles, this lighter-than-air craft was so huge that if placed on end it would have reached higher than a 75-story skyscraper! The *Macon* sank off Point Sur in February of 1935, and to this day this "dinosaur of the skies" rests on the bottom of the Pacific, along with four Curtiss Sparrowhawk airplanes that she carried in her hull.

Among the many seagoing vessels that have been lost off Point Sur are the coastal steamers *Ventura* (lost April 20, 1875) and *Los Angeles* (lost April 21, 1894). These wrecks are often referred to as "twin" shipwrecks because of the many similarities between them. Both vessels were retired government ships, both had been renovated for passenger service, and both were owned by the Pacific Coast Steamship Company. In addition, both mishaps were due to the negligence of the ship's officers, both wrecks occurred near Point Sur (one slightly to the north,

54

one slightly to the south), and both accidents took place in the month of April, within a day of each other, at approximately the same time of night, nineteen years apart.

Of additional interest to history buffs is information indicating that survivors of both wrecks were cared for by coastal residents and that in both cases the "spoils" (in the form of furnishings, linens, draperies, wool, 150 calves, and a large assortment of foodstuffs) were put to good use by the locals. Also washed ashore from the *Ventura* were a number of "knockdown wagons" (wagons that could be easily assembled and disassembled) that citizens of the Sur put together and used for many years. Ghost buffs will be interested in knowing that, according to old-timers, the sounds of the *Ventura's* "knockdown wagons" can sometimes still be heard in the Santa Lucias.

Certainly the strangest—and most ghostly—of the many shipwrecks in this area is the one that claimed the 3,000-ton coastal freighter *Babinda*. This aged wooden vessel caught fire off Monterey Bay's north shore in the early morning hours of March 3, 1923. The *Babinda's* crew fought the flames until it became obvious that the battle was lost. Thinking that the burning freighter was not long for this world, the crew abandoned ship and were picked up by the steamer *Celilo*, which transported them to the port of San Francisco.

But the *Babinda* was far from dead. Eerily, the vessel seemed to take on a new life after her crew departed and, almost as if she had a mind of her own, she began her last—and certainly her most dramatic—voyage. With clouds of smoke billowing from her hold, the *Babinda* drifted south past the populous Monterey Peninsula, past the treacherous Point Lobos promontory, and down the rugged Big Sur coast. Finally, more than a day after she had been abandoned, the *Babinda* slipped beneath the waves of Point Sur at 7:10 A.M. on March 4, 1923.

Who guided the old freighter on her farewell journey? Many of those who are familiar with the story say that the *Babinda* was commanded by a phantom skipper and manned by a ghostly crew as she worked her way approximately forty miles down the central California coast. Upon reaching his destination, they say, the spectral skipper let his vessel die a dignified and fitting death amid the bones of all the other vessels whose remains rest peacefully in Point Sur's Pacific graveyard of ships.*

"Somebody should do something for the lady in the next room . . ."

Those who cherish Big Sur's magnificent vistas might well envy the lightkeepers who have kept their lonely vigil on the promontory of Point Sur. Perched above the Point's historic lighthouse is the lightkeeper's three-story residence. Built of stone, the house can be seen from Highway One when the fog hasn't engulfed the distant rock. From this lonely outpost, one can look out on the dramatic meeting of land and sea that has made the Sur famous around the world.

Many tales are told about the small cluster of buildings that share the flat atop Point Sur. Among them are accounts of a teenage girl who died in her third-floor room in the lightkeeper's house—and whose ghost is said to haunt the bedroom to this day.

Even though I've heard several stories about the ghost, they all are similar in describing the sounds of coughing that come from a bedroom on the top floor. According to those who have checked into the story, in the early 1900s

*Those who would like more information about the shipwrecks discussed in this section—and many more—may wish to consult my book *Shipwrecks and Sea Monsters of California's Central Coast.*

this room was occupied by a young lady of about eighteen. Sadly, the girl suffered from consumption (also known as tuberculosis) and was often overcome by fits of coughing. (I can only imagine the damp coastal fog that often hovered over the Point didn't help matters.) Gradually the disease worsened, and the teenage miss died.

There the story might have ended, except for the strangely similar incidents that have been reported in the years since the girl's death. I will share two of these accounts here.

The first tale comes from a past lightkeeper who lived in the house with his family long after the teenager died. The family's eight-year-old son occupied the room next to the one in which the girl had died years before. Even though the boy knew nothing of her death, on several occasions he came downstairs complaining that he couldn't sleep because a lady (or girl) in the next room kept coughing! As you might expect, no one was in the room at the time.

This story is interesting in itself, but it becomes even more striking in light of an event that occurred several years later. The lightkeeper's house was being reroofed at the time. One night one of the roofers spent the night in the house. The room he stayed in was the same room that had belonged to the eight-year-old boy. Upon venturing downstairs the next morning, the worker—who knew nothing about the history of the house—remarked, "If it isn't already too late, somebody should do something for the lady in the next room because she has a terrible cough!" Needless to say, the worker didn't know the room was empty.

So there you have it, two incidents reported by different sources, taking place years apart and telling much the same story. As far as I know, no one has ever seen the girl's ghost, but several people claim to have heard her coughing. Were the sounds they heard really coming from the teenage miss, or were they caused by some peculiarity of the house? I'll let you be the judge, but consider this: Those who have spent the night in the room next to hers did not say they had heard a strange sound that was *something like* a cough. Instead, they were convinced that someone—most likely a young lady—was in the next room, keeping them awake with her coughing.

A tear-shaped ball of fire . . .

South of Point Sur, Highway One soon turns inland and heads for the beautiful Big Sur Valley. This is the heart of the Big Sur country, and it is here that the road passes through groves of redwood trees, skirts secluded campgrounds, and meanders past world-class resorts, exclusive inns, and weekend retreats favored by the rich and famous. Restaurants, motels, souvenir shops, delicatessens, grocery outlets, and a gas station or two also line the road. Most of these establishments welcome both visitors and locals, which is different from the days (mostly during the 1960s) when the hippies claimed the Sur as their own. A small post office and a county library branch (tucked away in a trailer) can also be found along the road in opposite directions from the entrance to the popular Pfeiffer Big Sur State Park, which is nestled in the heart of the valley.

It is on this inland stretch that Highway One crosses over the picturesque Big Sur River, named Rio Grande del Sur (Big River of the South) by the Spanish. Submerged rocks near the river's mouth were the site of another shipwreck of note, as the 405-foot Japanese freighter *Rhine Maru* met its end on this shore one dark and foggy night in 1930.

The Big Sur River plays a prominent part in our next tale, which takes us back to the days of World War II. As you know, during the 1940s many of California's Japanese-Americans were forced out of their homes and

58

into concentration camps. It was at one of these camps that a Monterey man (who was approaching sixty) and a teenager from Watsonville (on the opposite side of Monterey Bay) became close friends. After the Japanese returned to their homes following the war, the two men again planted their roots. As time went on, they lost contact with each other.

One day in the late 1940s, the Watsonville man was leading a group of Boy Scouts on a Big Sur outing. While hiking along the Big Sur River, he saw "a tear-shaped ball of fire" bobbing in the water. According to the fellow who told me this tale, the Japanese have a word for this phenomenon, which usually is associated with death. When the scout leader saw the fireball, his thoughts turned to his wartime friend, and he felt a tremendous desire to see him. Placing the scouts under the watchful eye of a second troop leader, he hurried to his car and raced to the home of his Monterey friend. Fearing the worst, the scout leader hesitantly knocked on the door, only to learn that his friend had died a few hours before.

Filled with grief at the news of his friend's passing, the scout leader remembered the mysterious ball of fire. It was then that he realized his wartime buddy's death had occurred at—or very near—the time he saw the fireball floating in the river!

As strange as this tale may sound, it comes from a source very close to the event. It was told to me by the son of the man who died. It was he who answered the door and broke the sad news of his father's death to the scout leader.

A ghostly knocking on their door and windows . . .

Our next tale takes us south of the Big Sur Valley and up a long grade. At the top of the grade we come to an old house on the inland side of the road. Even though it sags a bit here and there, and certainly shows signs of wear, the building is still quite attractive and is one of the Sur's most familiar landmarks. Built in the 1860s, and added onto a decade later, it is known to old-timers simply as "Posts," as it was the headquarters of the historic Post Ranch, also of 1860s vintage. Not only did five generations of the Post family live there, but it also served as Big Sur's first "continuously operated" post office.

Among the many stories associated with this house is one that tells about the ghost of a young man of Mexican descent. The young man had worked as a ranch hand for the Post family. He is reported to have shared one of the building's back rooms with some of his fellow workers.

One day while he was riding a horse in a nearby canyon, he was thrown from his mount and killed. After lamenting the loss of the likable lad, the occupants of the house began hearing familiar—and most discomforting— "noises in the night." Among the sounds were those of footsteps on the back porch and rapping noises on the back door and windows, as if someone was seeking entry. The trouble was, there was no one to be seen outside.

The people in the house felt sure that the young man's ghost had returned. Frantically, they searched through the room in which he had stayed, hoping to find something that his ghost might be seeking. Upon finding three "store-bought collars" that had been prized by the lad, they quickly threw them out. From that moment on they were never again troubled by the frightening sounds of footsteps and a ghostly knocking on their door and windows.*

---

*For those reading this book while traveling south on Highway One, the Post house is at the top of the "Post Grade" (approximately three miles south of the Pfeiffer Big Sur State Park entrance). The turnoffs to two of the Sur's most popular resort inns are in the same area of the highway, on opposite sides of the road.

He was immediately aware of his departed friend's presence . . .

Upon topping the Post Grade and starting down the other side, we pass a number of local landmarks, including the renowned restaurant and watering spot known as Nepenthe (Greek for "no sorrow"). Opened in 1949, this popular gathering place—with its multimillion-dollar view—has attracted visitors from around the globe. Of interest to history buffs is information indicating that the site was "discovered" by those of name and fame even before it became a restaurant, as the cabin that was originally built there was once owned by Rita Hayworth and Orson Welles. (Hmm, I wonder if their ghosts might still be about?)

After passing Nepenthe and continuing down the grade, we come to the Henry Miller Memorial Library, located in a small house that was once owned by Miller's good friend Emil White. Did you know that this famed writer (author of such books as *Tropic of Cancer* and *Tropic of Capricorn,* and my favorite, *Big Sur and the Oranges of Hieronymus Bosch),* was a Big Sur resident for many years? Miller lived in the area—mostly atop Partington Ridge—from the mid 1940s to the early 1960s.

Another bend or two brings us to a rustic coastal inn, a place that to many—at least in its early days—represented the essence of Big Sur. Nestled in a canyon, and blending with the redwoods and a brisk mountain stream, this roadside retreat had its beginning before Highway One was completed and today looks back on many years of memories.

Uppermost among these memories, at least for those who knew the inn in decades past, are the times shared with Papa—the man who created this magical place. Unfortunately, Papa passed away in 1972. However, even though the spirit behind this "spot time forgot" no longer holds court at the long table inside the board-and-batten barn (where the restaurant is now located), both residents and visitors who have long been a part of this Big Sur experience have reported seeing and feeling his presence.

Dressed in his usual attire—complete with suspenders—Papa usually appeared only to those he knew. In his own special way, he added a "difficult to describe" feeling of warmth and goodwill to the many other positive experiences that are shared by a select group of guests who have long frequented the inn. Most of these "regulars" have spent the night among the memorabilia in "Papa's room."

One incident *not* of the positive variety took place in Papa's room in the late 1970s. Even though it is the only happening of its kind that has ever been reported (at least to my knowledge), I find it of more than passing interest, in part because of the innkeeper's intuition even before the event took place. As he described to me when we chatted several years ago, early one afternoon when he was raking leaves near Papa's room, he looked up to see a young couple being escorted to the cabin-like quarters. Upon glancing at the pair, the innkeeper (who had been one of Papa's most trusted friends) had a strange feeling of doubt about the couple and whether they were "right for the room." However, when they appeared happy and excited about their lodgings, he shrugged off his concern and continued with his chores.

As evening approached and the inn's cozy restaurant became crowded with guests and good cheer, the innkeeper acted as host to those who partook of the excellent food, the classical music, and the warmth of the facility's many fireplaces. Along about 9:30, as the evening began to mellow, the phone suddenly rang, its jarring tones spoiling the ambiance of the night. Upon answering the call, the innkeeper felt his original doubts come back to haunt him, as on the line was the man who had registered to stay in Papa's room. Calling from a second location, the troubled man said that he and his wife had left "in a hurry," and that they wouldn't be spending the night after all. In continuing, he reported that in their haste to get out of the room they had left some of their belongings, which they would return for in the morning.

More than a little concerned about what had taken place, the innkeeper hurried across the yard to Papa's room. When he reached the cabin, he was both surprised and annoyed to find the lights on, the door open, and the couple's things scattered about.

Upon entering the room to turn the lights out, he was immediately aware of Papa's presence. Not only was the feeling of presence stronger than he had ever experienced it before, but he also sensed that Papa wanted to be left alone. With the message being very clear, the innkeeper excused himself, bade Papa good night, turned off the lights, and quietly closed the door.

Early the next morning the couple returned for their belongings. Not only did they not mention what had taken place to drive them away, but they didn't even ask for their money back! Several years after the event, when the innkeeper shared this account with me, he still had difficulty explaining what it was about the couple that made him wonder if they were "right for the room." However, he did take satisfaction in knowing that whatever it was that had made him have doubts about the pair, it was obviously shared by his long departed friend—the grand old man who had built the inn.

With all other experiences of the supernatural kind having been of the positive variety, and with Papa posthumously approving of the way things were being run, all indications pointed to many more years of happiness and success for this "up the creek and under the redwoods" Big Sur retreat.

The clock was keeping perfect time . . .

As we continue south on Highway One, and away from the redwood-lined canyon where Papa once held court, the mighty Santa Lucias and the rugged Pacific shoreline again command our view. In marveling at these majestic mountains and their sheer drop into the sea, it's hard not to imagine what the scene must have been like before humans scarred the landscape with dynamite and dump trucks, and built a monument to a motorized public in the form of the magnificent coast highway. Today there are few old-timers who can remember what it was like before this thin cement line linked the north with the south, and one must work fast if he wishes to record their recollections of the way it used to be. Other than old-timers and their treasure trove of memories, about all that is left for historians to ponder are faded photographs, musty diaries, forgotten letters, yellowed newspapers, and a scattering of books.

It is this thought that brings me to our next tale, as it was an account from an aged newspaper (found in the scrapbook of a pioneer Monterey County resident) that brought to light the story of a crude south coast shack and a clock that wouldn't quit.

Published many years ago, the article tells of a 40-acre parcel of land—complete with cabin—that was being offered for sale. The author of the article told how he hiked to the isolated acreage with a companion. Upon reaching the weathered building (located at a height of about 1,000 feet and approximately a half-mile from the ocean), both he and his partner were surprised at the way Mother Nature had reclaimed the structure's fenced-in yard. After climbing over the decrepit fence, the pair made their way to the front of the cabin. On reaching the rickety steps that led to the dwelling's only door, they patiently unwound the rusty wire that held the door shut and entered the structure.

As they cautiously crept into the long-vacant building, they were startled to hear the sound of a clock loudly ticking. The clock was of the old-fashioned variety and had to be hand wound. It was obvious that no one was about to wind the clock. Yet not only was the clock running, but a check of their own watches showed that all three timepieces showed the exact same time!

The astonished visitors spent the better part of an hour in and about the abandoned shack, satisfying themselves that the dwelling hadn't been entered for many years. Finally, upon taking their leave, they again checked the clock and found that not only was it ticking as loudly as ever, but it was also keeping perfect time!

As they began their long walk away from the cabin, the somewhat shaken pair reported a distinct—and disturbing—feeling of presence, almost as if they were being watched. It was this information that prompted certain local residents to think of the oft-told tales of the Santa Lucia's mysterious dark watchers. Could these strange beings—or perhaps Una Jeffers' "little people"—have settled in the vicinity of the lonely mountain shack, where they watched over and wound the aged clock?

If you want to stretch your imagination even further, could there be some element in the earth that somehow affected the cabin's old timepiece? As strange as this may seem, it is said that there are places in the Sur (such as Pfeiffer Point, west of the Post Ranch homestead) that contain iron ore in large enough quantities to deflect a ship's compass. Could this be why the 839-ton steam schooner *Shna-Yak* went aground off Pfeiffer Point during a dense fog in 1916, only to be followed by the 657-ton lumber schooner *Thomas L. Wand*, also during a dense fog, six years later?

While we're wondering, I wonder whether the cabin with the clock is still there. I wonder whether the clock is still running, and whether it's on Standard or Daylight Savings time. But most of all, I wonder whether the author of the article that started this discussion simply made the whole thing up!

Suddenly, hundreds of poppies opened . . .

As I sit on a ridge gazing at the coastal mountains, I'm reminded of another tale that falls into the category of the strange and unexplained. The exact location of this incident is unimportant, as I do know that it took place along the Big Sur coast.

This story was told to me by a friend of the man who experienced it. The man had been involved in a one-sided love affair. Although the woman of his dreams was a close friend, she did not feel the same fondness for him that he felt for her. Remaining a bachelor, the man lived his life longing for the lady he couldn't have.

As the years passed, the woman became ill. Upon learning of her illness the man became greatly depressed. One day, feeling sad and lonely, he took a walk in a field. The day was dreary and heavy with fog, and as he walked he became lost in thought. Suddenly, hundreds of poppies that were scattered about the field opened as if it were a bright sunny day! After remaining open for a few seconds, the poppies then closed as if it were night.

The man had no idea what the significance of this beautiful event might be until he learned later that the love of his life had died—at the precise moment the poppies had opened!

The skulls seemed to stare at them through eyeless holes . . .

Beyond the field of poppies, and beyond a spot known to locals as Lover's Leap (where a long-ago lady who had been jilted by her lover is said to have jumped to her death, and where her mournful cries can still be heard on certain dark and foggy nights), we come to the site of Massacre Cave. Perhaps best known to gold seekers who comb the adjoining Santa Lucias, Massacre Cave harbors a chilling secret—one that has baffled historians and law enforcement officers for many years.

Massacre Cave is located on a steep Santa Lucia slope only a short distance from Highway One, and even closer to Willow Creek (slightly north of Cape San Martin). The sealed entrance to this cave of death was stumbled upon by three gold seekers from the San Francisco area in 1962. It happened like this. After a long and tiring day of placer mining in and around Willow Creek, the threesome were resting on the banks of the stream when they noticed a number of bats seemingly flying in and out of a nearby mountainside.

Wondering whether the tiny opening the bats had discovered could be the sealed entrance of a larger cave (such as the famed Lost Padre Mine), the gold seekers worked their way up the sloping peak. Finding a tiny aperture in the rock, the eager argonauts shooed away the bats and settled down to serious digging. After about an hour of energetic work they managed to clear an opening large enough to squeeze through.

As the cave opened up, the gruesome sight that greeted the first visitor is one that will long remain etched in his memory. Scattered about the rocky, uneven floor were the remains of several long-dead human beings!

After a quick exploration, the cave—which initially appeared to contain only one small room—was found to have multiple chambers at varying depths. Twenty feet inside the entrance a drop of fifteen feet was discovered. Lowering themselves down the drop, the intrepid explorers found still a third level, taking them ever deeper into their chamber of horror.

As the beams of their flashlights pierced the eerie darkness, the men saw more skeletons strewn about on all levels, the skulls seeming to stare at them through eyeless holes. Shivering, the men spotted additional rooms and tiny passageways off the lower chamber, but large boulders blocked their entrances.

After the initial shock wore off, the gold seekers counted at least ten human skeletons! Dumbfounded by their gruesome discovery, the shaken argonauts wisely notified authorities. Soon the press learned of the find, and it was they who dubbed the site Massacre Cave. An anthropologist from one of California's leading universities, together with sheriff's deputies, the county coroner, and representatives of the media, hustled to the scene to inspect the grim remains.

After careful study, nine of the skulls were identified as Indian, with the tenth being of European origin (possibly Spanish). An "educated guess" placed the time of the deaths at about 1860—approximately 100 years before they were found. Adding to the grisly nature of the find, most of the skulls showed signs of having been cracked, "as if by a blunt instrument."

Speculation about who might have committed the century-old murders was soon running rampant. Thoughts of what may have happened came from several sources. One of the tales stems from an early Carmel Mission legend. Briefly, this account tells about a lost gold mine that was worked by the mission Indians. Like Massacre Cave, the mine was said to be in the Santa Lucia Mountains south of the church.

As the story goes, Spanish soldiers from the Monterey Presidio stumbled upon the mine. Excited about the find, they forced the Indians into continuing their work while they pocketed the profits. Upon being relieved of their California duties, the soldiers allegedly killed the Indians and sealed their bodies in the mine. In this way they hoped to keep the mine's location a secret. Perhaps the Indians killed one of the soldiers in the process, which would explain the lone European.

Several bits of information lend credence to this tale, with, perhaps, the most important being that a lot of gold has been found in the Santa Lucia Mountains near Massacre Cave! Unfortunately, the anthropologist's estimate that the deaths took place around 1860 doesn't fit with this theory, since the Spanish soldiers had been relieved of their California duties long before then.

A number of other accounts have been offered about Massacre Cave, but the mystery of the apparent murders remains unsolved. Whatever the explanation may be, it takes little imagination to sense the presence of numerous ghostly spirits (and Indian curses) lingering around this cave of death.

The Headless Horselady of Mission San Antonio . . .

The mention of gold seekers in the preceding account leads us to the rich history (rich in more ways than one) of the Santa Lucia Mountains. Did you know that at one time there was a gold rush in these mountains? That hundreds of thousands of dollars' worth of gold was taken from the coastal peaks? That a mining town that once boasted hundreds of residents once stood on a flat in the middle of the mining district? And that an enormous amount of gold is *still* waiting to be found?

The mining district in question was the Los Burros Mining District, which was founded in 1875. However, gold played a part in the colorful history of south Monterey County long before that. Among the more persistent of the early gold seekers were the Chinese, many of whom were drifters from the Sierra Nevada. Documents indicate that these seekers of fortune were placer mining on the eastern slopes of the Santa Lucias in the early 1850s. Twenty years later, with more and more miners (mostly of the hard-rock variety) finding their way to this coastal Mother Lode, it became obvious that some sort of rules— mining justice, if you will—were needed. Thus, the district was formed.

Interestingly, even though a town sprang up (similar to mining camps throughout the Sierras), and mines were being claimed faster than they could be recorded (with over 2,000 claims eventually being registered), the best paying mine wasn't discovered until 1887. Known as the Last Chance Mine, it produced tens of thousands of dollars' worth of gold (as recorded by the United States Bureau of Mines). Its shaft flooded before the true extent of its wealth could be realized.

The town continued to boom, boasting such things as a hotel, two general stores, a post office, a barber shop, a butcher shop, a blacksmith shop, a confectionery shop, a restaurant, a one-room school, numerous miners' cabins, and, of course, a dance hall and a number of saloons. The town was best known as Manchester, although its name was changed to Mansfield with the coming of the post office in 1889. It succumbed to fire around the turn of the twentieth century. Today the town, which is frequently referred to as "The Lost City of the Santa Lucias," is truly a ghost of the past.

The mention of ghosts brings me to one of my favorite tales connected with gold mining in Monterey County. Not only does it take us back to the early days of mining in the Santa Lucias, but it tells of an Indian woman who literally lost her head over an affair with a local miner. As the aged account goes, the woman was in the habit of slipping away from her husband (as well as other Indians who still lived in the area of the decaying Mission San Antonio, located near the tiny town of Jolon) and spending time with a prospector in the nearby hills.*

---

*Jolon was the "jumping-off place" for pack trains heading for Los Burros. Mission San Antonio was the third church in Father Junipero Serra's chain of California missions and was founded in 1771. For ghost stories and other odd happenings connected with this church, see my books *Ghostly Tales and Mysterious Happenings of Old Monterey, Ghost Notes,* and *California Ghost Notes.*

Unfortunately for the woman, her husband caught her and the prospector together. In a jealous rage he killed her and chopped her head off with an axe! When this was accomplished, he buried her body in one grave and her decapitated head in another.

With this grisly account serving as background, and with added information indicating that many of the local Indians believed that a body must be buried intact before it can lie at rest, one does not have to stretch his imagination far to realize that the famed "headless horselady" of the Mission San Antonio area is, in all probability, the unfaithful Indian woman in an eternal search for her head.

In days of old, residents of nearby communities as well as those who lived on ranches and farms in the valleys and hills of the easterly Santa Lucias, were aware of the legend of the headless horselady and her never-ending search for her lost head. The majority of the old-timers attributed the sightings of the headless rider to hallucinations of the Indians when they were under the influence of peyote powder. (Peyote powder was obtained from mescal cactuses. It is described as an intoxicating drug.)

Nevertheless, researchers wondered whether there was any truth to the tale and made several attempts to talk to descendants of Indians who long ago lived and worked in the San Antonio area. In tracking these people down and asking them about the aged account, the researchers learned that the descendants preferred not to comment on the story.

With the Indians not wishing to discuss the tale, and with most of the old-timers being of the opinion that the sightings were nothing more than drug-induced visions, the story would probably have died a natural death if several sightings had not been made in the 1960s and 70s.

The revival of the headless horselady tales were mostly credited to soldiers who were standing duty at various lonely guard posts in Fort Hunter Liggett, a vast military complex that surrounds Mission San Antonio and extends into the Santa Lucia Mountains. The majority of the sightings are said to have been made in the early morning hours in an area of Hunter Liggett known as the ammo supply point (ASP).

One such sighting describes the headless figure as riding a horse along a nearby crest of mountains. Referring to the woman as Cleora (Kli-or-ah), the bewildered soldier went on to say, "I saw it while at ASP in December (1974). It was a female, I'm sure of that." Pointing to his neck, the soldier added, "And there was nothing from here up!"

In another ammo supply point account, a second soldier, who was also standing guard duty, told of seeing a headless figure approaching. When the figure disregarded his command to halt, the soldier drew his weapon—only to have the ghostly image vanish into the night.

A third incident involves a soldier who was on guard duty in a small building near what is known as the Gabilan impact area. Upon hearing a knock on the door he challenged the visitor but received no answer. Cautiously going out of the building to see what was going on, he was unable to find anyone—or anything out of the ordinary. It was after he was back in the building and peering out a window that he saw the headless figure of a woman wearing a cape (or overcoat) and long flowing robes!

Brother Anthony (not his real name), who spent many years at Mission San Antonio, was somewhat of a student of history, and was very interested in the tales of the headless horselady as well as other stories about the area. He would nod knowingly when accounts of the headless rider were brought up, and, upon occasion, he would add a tale or two himself. During one of our talks (in the 1970s) he remarked, "Over the years *several* people have reported seeing or hearing the headless horsewoman as she rides by the church."

It was Brother Anthony who told of four MPs who came to him in January of 1975 swearing that they had not only seen the ghostly apparition, but had actually chased her and her spirited mount with their jeeps, only to lose her as she disappeared into the wilderness.

I could go on with headless horselady stories, but as we are getting away from Los Burros, and even farther from the coast, perhaps I should leave additional research to you and return to the legends and lore of Monterey County's gold country.

"Earth-bound spirits" frequented the mine . . .

The Los Burros Mining District, like gold mining regions everywhere, boasts numerous unsolved mysteries and tales of intrigue. Who stashed those bodies in Massacre Cave? Was the legendary Lost Padre Mine in the Los Burros territory? Who were the miners who secretly dug a "whopping" 300-foot tunnel toward the heart of the district's best paying mine—and then sealed its entrance? What accounts for the visions of mountain men wearing dark jackets, slouch hats, and beards that hid their faces? What secret lies behind the mysterious disappearance of the first recorder of claims, followed by his son (the founder of the famed Last Chance Mine) thirty years later?

Yes, mysteries abound about Los Burros, with many of them involving its hearty pioneers, strong men with even stronger wills, men who blazed the trails and staked the claims. That's one reason why the story of the Ghost of Gold mine intrigues me so. You see, this claim was owned and worked by a woman! As if this isn't almost unheard of on its own (at least in Los Burros), the fact that this "miniature miner" also owned (or had part interest in) nearly two dozen other claims makes this account of even more interest. Holding her own, and not pushed around by anyone, this mountain miss also owned her own bulldozer, as well as a jeep, and when it came to hard work she put many of her fellow gold seekers to shame.

Such a woman was clearly not one to be easily spooked. Yet it was she who told of having been frightened by unnatural happenings in and around her Ghost of Gold claim. In describing her experiences, she spoke somewhat hesitatingly about "earth-bound spirits" that frequented the mine. In addition to the ghostly spirits, she told of a strange wolf-like creature that she had observed in the area, and of aged automobiles that were often heard—but never seen—as they chugged along the road and through the nearby trees.

With these sightings, feelings, and sounds all being very real to our rugged mountain miss, and with the story having become fairly well known, several people attempted to solve the mysteries with logical explanations. The sounds of the chugging automobiles, they suggested, may have been nothing more than the sounds of diesel-powered freighters as they plied the waters of the distant Pacific (although the ships would have been many miles away). Because there are no wolves in Monterey County, the wolf-like creature was described as a possible descendant of an escapee from the William Randolph Hearst zoo of Hearst Castle fame, located in the San Luis Obispo County section of the Santa Lucias.

However logical, or illogical, these explanations may be, they do offer some sort of solutions to two of the Ghost of Gold's mysteries. This brings us to the "earth-bound spirits" that frightened our lady miner. As no one has managed to explain these spirits, the fact that they were very real to our no-nonsense Los Burros lass makes them *logical* candidates for our ever-expanding list of ghostly happenings that occur in and around beautiful Big Sur.

A Hearst Castle haunting . . .

Even though it stretches our coverage beyond what is generally thought of as Big Sur, with my mention of Hearst

Castle in the last account I'd like to end this book with a brief ghost story about this remarkable place. As you probably know, Hearst Castle sits high on a hill overlooking the Pacific Ocean, approximately twelve miles south of the Monterey/San Luis Obispo County line. This impressive edifice was the "country home" of William Randolph Hearst. The son of George Hearst, a mining magnate and United States Senator, the younger Hearst was perhaps best known as a publisher of many of the nation's leading newspapers and magazines. In addition, he owned movie companies and radio stations, along with immense tracts of land in both the United States and Mexico. Politics were another of his interests, as from 1903 to 1907 he represented New York in the U.S. House of Representatives.

Hearst Castle, as his palatial California retreat came to be called, was one of the most imposing private dwellings in America. Its furnishings (collected from around the world) were, if possible, even more imposing than its exterior. Prior to Hearst's death in 1951, the "Enchanted Hill" (upon which the castle was built) and its surrounding land (which totaled about 240,000 acres—including fifty miles of ocean frontage!) were a gathering place for the rich and famous. Other than numerous Hollywood celebrities, other people of note who visited this "country estate" were such luminaries as United States President Calvin Coolidge and the beloved British statesman and writer Winston Churchill.

Interestingly, while books have been written about the castle and the man who built it (not to mention his famous architect, Julia Morgan), relatively little is known about the structure's ghosts. Over the years, numerous tales have circulated about apparitions and other odd goings-on, yet the majority of the accounts were never recorded. At least that's the word I got from the guides and docents who work at the site, and who declined to discuss the events. (As you may know, Hearst Castle is now owned by the state and is open to the public on a guided tour basis.)

Pursuing my quest for ghost stories connected with the castle, I tried to seek out an old-timer a teacher friend of mine had told me about. This man had not only helped build the mansion, but had also worked there for many years. Rumor had it that he knew several ghostly tales about "The Hill." Unfortunately, by the time I was able to track him down, he had recently died. According to his son, who himself was elderly, his dad had never written down any of the accounts. Sad to learn of the old man's passing, I went on with my life, resigned to the fact that ghost stories about Hearst Castle were destined to remain elusive.

Then, one day in 1994, a Hearst Castle ghost story came to me "out of the blue." I was at a reading conference in Oakland, California, where I was scheduled to give a talk and sign and sell books. There I met a young teacher whom I will call Bonnie. On the first day of the conference, Bonnie and I had a brief chat about ghosts, and how I did my research, before she had to run off to her next session. The next day, she returned. This time, however, her mood soon became quite serious. When she and I were alone, she somewhat self-consciously told me that when she was twelve she had had a ghostly experience when she visited Hearst Castle with her family. That said, she began to get teary-eyed and quickly changed the subject.

A few minutes later, having regained her composure, Bonnie resumed telling me about the Hearst Castle happening. Everything was fine, she related, until the tour group her family was with entered the master bedroom. It was there that she saw the ghostly figure of an older woman in the large bed! As the group continued to filter into the room, the lady—who appeared to have been sleeping—sat up in bed and watched the people. Upon spotting Bonnie she smiled and indicated that she wanted her to come closer. Knowing that the bed was off-limits (as visitors weren't allowed to go into the roped-off sections of the rooms), and not knowing who the lady was, Bonnie chose to stay with her family and the rest of the group. However, the whole time they were there Bonnie stared at the woman, who continued to smile and beckon her to come nearer.

When the tour leader finished talking about the bedroom and its priceless furnishings, the group followed him to the next stop. As soon as they filed out of the bedroom, Bonnie asked her father if he had seen the lady. As it turned out, neither he—nor anyone else in her family— had seen the apparition!

Bonnie concluded by saying that she had continued to be bothered by the sighting ever since. Who was the lady in the bed? Why was she visible only to her? And why did she continue to gesture to her to come closer? Years after the experience, the questions—and the mystery—lingered.

In listening to Bonnie's account, and observing how emotional she became when she told me the tale, I was touched by her sincerity, and I believe that I am one of only a few people with whom she has shared this experience.

It is stories like these, related by sincere and sober individuals, that make me believe there's *something* to at least some of the tales of ghosts and other strange happenings that continue to circulate around Big Sur, as well as countless other places. I'm certain Bonnie believed there was *someone* in that bed! Why was she the only one who was able to see the apparition? I don't know, but after more than thirty years of collecting ghost stories, I'm of the opinion that we must be open to such happenings before we can experience them. Maybe, at twelve, Bonnie was one of those chosen ones—someone whose mind was not already made up—while others on the tour (her family included) had already closed their minds to ghosts . . . and to things that go bump in the night.

Afterword

I think all who are familiar with the Big Sur region will agree that it would be impossible in a book of this size to include all the accounts of ghosts or mysterious happenings that are associated with Monterey County's scenic south shore. In fact, this book doesn't even include all of the stories I am personally aware of. Among the accounts I have purposely left out are a number of tales that are well known to old-timers. Because they may have rekindled sad memories for some of these folk, I chose to omit them from this narrative. There comes a time when it's best to let the ghosts rest.

In regard to the book's authenticity, I can only say that at times there is a fine line between fact and fiction, and often the two overlap. I'm certain that this is the case with this publication. However, when research was possible the facts were substantiated. That said, I must admit that when it comes to such things as ghostly sightings, feelings of presence, dark watchers, and runaway wagons (to mention only a few), I could only record what was reported to me. I will leave the final verdict up to you as to what is real and what may have been imagined.

Those who desire more in the way of Big Sur lore may do well to seek out a psychic, as some of these folk are of the opinion that certain sections of the Sur are "centers" for "psychic forces." One such individual even indicated that there was a UFO "launching pad" and "port of entry" off Point Sur. Certainly, something of the sort might help to explain the multiple shipwrecks, the compass variations, the UFO sightings, the singed ring of grass, and a host of other odd events that have occurred in this area— provided, of course, that the explanation has a basis in fact. Another psychic of note described Point Lobos as "the center of psychic force for the entire Pacific Coast." Again, if she is right, this privileged status may help to explain the myriad of other peculiar happenings that have taken place along the Monterey County coast. Maybe these "psychic forces" (whatever they may be) are also somehow related to the "haunted groves" of cypress trees that abound at Point Lobos (as described by still another psychic). Hmm, if so, I wonder whether these trees have anything to do with the ghost that haunts the old Whaler's Cabin at Point Lobos? Or maybe the spirit that drifts through the cabin each night about twelve is the ghost of a long-ago Spaniard who was killed at the site and then buried beneath the floor . . .

Yes, there are many stories that remain untold, and many mysteries that remain unsolved. If you decide to tramp the back trails of the Santa Lucias or explore the Big Sur shore looking for answers, then please do me a favor. If you see the dark watchers, give them my best, and if you run across the cabin with the clock, let me know if it's still keeping time . . .

Acknowledgments

As with most books that report incidents involving ghosts and peculiar happenings, a considerable amount of research was required in the preparation of this publication. This research takes many forms, including the seeking out of diaries, letters, scrapbooks, and assorted other documents that were created by the residents of the region. Other information often comes from an assortment of publications—newspapers included—that recount odd occurrences and strange goings-on. However, the most valuable, the most enjoyable, and certainly the most rewarding part of the research consists of tracking down the people who reside in the locale being studied, and in listening to their stories.

As I think about the many individuals who have shared their experiences with me—not to mention the information I gained when I worked as a Big Sur Park attendant during my college years—I must admit that, in a roundabout way, the research for this book began a *long* time ago. When I was a lad growing up in Monterey, my father, A. M. (Reiny) Reinstedt, made regular trips down the Big Sur coast before the highway was completed. His job was to deliver Standard Oil products to the people of the Sur. As I grew to adulthood, my dad told me many fascinating tales about the people, the places, and the happenings associated with this region. For these reasons—and more—I have dedicated this book to my father, and to his many south coast friends. Their stories are as much a part of the history of this wilderness land as are the trees, the mountains, and the rugged shore.

Unfortunately, it is impossible to acknowledge every individual who has contributed, directly or indirectly, to this work, in some cases because their accounts were told in the dim and distant past, long before any names were taken or thoughts were given to a publication of this type. Nevertheless, I don't think it would be right to publish this book without acknowledging at least some of the people who have helped along the way. So, hats off to Emily Brown, John Crisan Jr., Ed Gardien, Wil Goodrich, John Hayashida, Don Howard, Myrtle Leaman, Max and Otto Plapp, Jessie Sandholdt, Elizabeth Shields, Mary Sherman, Fred Sorri, Homer Stephens, Joe Victorine, and Ruby Woicekowski.

Among the many useful sources I consulted were *A Short History of Big Sur*, by Ronald Bostwick; *Big Sur*, by Tomi Kay Lussier; *Begin the Big Sur . . . at Palo Colorado Canyon*, by Charles Mohler; *Carmel Today and Yesterday*, by Daisy Bostick; *Monterey Coast Fifty-Five Years Ago*, written in 1941 by Dr. John L. D. Roberts ("The Father of the Coast Road"); *Sea Bells,* by John Fleming Wilson; *When the Coast Was Wild and Lonely*, by Rosalind Sharpe Wall; and numerous editions of the *Monterey Peninsula Herald* newspaper.

While the preceding people and sources played important parts in the preparation of this work, my most heartfelt thanks are reserved for my wife, Debbie, my son, Erick, his wife, Mary Ann, my editor, John Bergez, and my (now deceased) English bulldog, Joshua Jonas McCabe. Once again, these are the ones who bore the brunt of the many trials and tribulations of still another publication, and supported me all the way.

Photo Credits

This page constitutes an extension of the copyright page.

Pages 1, 5, 79, 81, 83. Notley's Landing, Bancroft Library Collection

Page 35: Carmelite Monastery (top), photo by L. Josselyn, P. Hathaway Collection; Whaler's Cove and inset (bottom), P. Hathaway Collection

Page 36: Notley's Landing (top), Bancroft Library Collection, inset by H. Lyons, P. Hathaway Collection; lumber mill and inset (bottom), photos by R. A. Reinstedt, R. A. Reinstedt Collection

Page 37: Monterey Lime Company and inset (top), P. Hathaway Collection; Bixby Point (bottom), photo by L. Josselyn, P. Hathaway Collection; inset, California State Library Collection

Page 38: Bixby Creek Bridge, main photo by L. Josselyn; both photos P. Hathaway Collection

Page 39: *Macon*, National Archives Collection #80-CF-4163-15; inset, Monterey Maritime Museum Collection

Page 40: Point Sur and inset (top), P. Hathaway Collection; Pico Blanco (bottom), photo by R. A. Reinstedt, R. A. Reinstedt Collection

Page 41: Clark cabin and inset (top), R. Woicekowski Collection; Post house (bottom), photo by L. Josselyn, P. Hathaway Collection

Page 42: Big Sur coast (top), photo by L. Josselyn, P. Hathaway Collection; Massacre Cave (bottom), photo by J. L. Crisan Jr., J. L. Crisan Jr. Collection

Page 43: Manchester, photo by M. Fisher, Monterey Savings & Loan Collection

Page 44: Gem Saloon (left), Monterey County Library Collection; Willie Cruikshank (right), Adrian Harbolt Collection

Books by Randall A. Reinstedt

Regional History and Lore Series . . .
bringing the colorful history of California's Central Coast to life for adults and older children

California Ghost Notes
From Fisherman's Wharf to Steinbeck's Cannery Row
Ghost Notes
Ghostly Tales and Mysterious Happenings of Old Monterey
Ghosts, Bandits and Legends of Old Monterey
Ghosts and Mystery Along Old Monterey's Path of History
Ghosts of the Big Sur Coast
Incredible Ghosts of Old Monterey's Hotel Del Monte
Monterey's Mother Lode
Mysterious Sea Monsters of California's Central Coast
Shipwrecks and Sea Monsters of California's Central Coast
Tales, Treasures and Pirates of Old Monterey

History & Happenings of California Series . . .
putting the story back in history for young readers

Lean John, California's Horseback Hero
One-Eyed Charley, the California Whip
Otters, Octopuses, and Odd Creatures of the Deep
Stagecoach Santa
The Strange Case of the Ghosts of the
    Robert Louis Stevenson House
Tales and Treasures of California's Missions
Tales and Treasures of California's Ranchos
Tales and Treasures of the California Gold Rush

For information on purchasing books contact:

Ghost Town Publications
P.O. Drawer 5998 ◆ Carmel, CA 93921 ◆ (831) 373-2885
www.ghosttownpub.com